ADVANCE PRAISE

CRY WOLF

Relationships with predators are complex and challenging in an increasingly human-dominated world. I know so because for 25 years I have lived with my family in a remote place where the predator population outnumbers the human population. While my relationships with these predators have been peaceful, that is not always the case. In this insightful book, Harold R. Johnson presents an insider's and First Nations' perspective on the Kenton Carnegie case. He eloquently argues that Traditional Ecological Knowledge and the wisdom of Indigenous people can help us better understand the true nature of predators such as wolves and live more peacefully with them.
—Cristina Eisenberg, PhD, author of
   The Wolf's Tooth and *The Carnivore Way*

CRY
WOLF
INQUEST INTO THE TRUE
NATURE OF A PREDATOR

HAROLD R. JOHNSON

 University of Regina Press

Printed and bound in Canada at Marquis. The text of this book is printed on
100% post-consumer recycled paper with earth-friendly vegetable-based inks.

Cover design: Duncan Campbell, University of Regina Press
Text design: John van der Woude, JVDW Designs
Copy editor: Alison Jacques
Proofreader: Dallas Harrison
Indexer: Siusan Moffat

Cover art: "Wolf in Winter," by mirceax / iStock by Getty Images
Photos pages 53 and 109: Pixabay.com

Library and Archives Canada Cataloguing in Publication

Title: Cry wolf : inquest into the true nature of a predator / Harold R.
    Johnson.
Names: Johnson, Harold, 1957- author.
Description: Includes bibliographical references and index.
Identifiers: Canadiana (print) 20190187778 | Canadiana (ebook)
    20190187808 | ISBN 9780889777385 (softcover) | ISBN 9780889777408
    (PDF) | ISBN 9780889777422 (HTML)
Subjects: LCSH: Carnegie, Kenton, 1983-2005. | LCSH: Wolf attacks—
    Saskatchewan—Case studies. | LCSH: Wolves—Behavior—Case studies. |
    LCGFT: Case studies.
Classification: LCC QL737.C22 J64 2020 | DDC 599.773—dc23

10 9 8 7 6 5 4 3 2 1

University of Regina Press, University of Regina
Regina, Saskatchewan, Canada, S4S 0A2
tel: (306) 585-4758 fax: (306) 585-4699
web: www.uofrpress.ca

We acknowledge the support of the Canada Council for the Arts for
our publishing program. We acknowledge the financial support of the
Government of Canada. / Nous reconnaissons l'appui financier du
gouvernement du Canada. This publication was made possible with support
from Creative Saskatchewan's Book Publishing Production Grant Program.

READER ADVISORY

The content of this book, including the writing and some of the images used, depicts violence and a violent death by wolf attack. Reader discretion is advised. Also, a warning that this book may not be suitable for young children.

Figure 1. Kenton Joel Carnegie (1983–2005) near the scene of his death. (Photograph courtesy of Coroner's Office, Government of Saskatchewan.)

TABLE OF CONTENTS

INTRODUCTION
THE TRUTH

If *Homo sapiens* are going to survive into the future, we need accurate information about our environment. We rely upon the government to make decisions and hope those decisions are based on the very best science available. But we know that governments are likely to make choices based more on popularity than on evidence. That's just the nature of our present system of elections and politics.

Scientists, on the other hand, don't have to be re-elected. They have a code for evaluating evidence, and we have become more trustful of scientists than politicians. We trust the scientific method to give us accurate answers.

But what happens when the government refuses to fund the necessary science? Or, even worse, when a scientist manipulates the data for political reasons? The following chapters outline what I saw in northern Saskatchewan surrounding the death of Kenton Joel Carnegie, a young man who went for a walk and never returned. His body was found a few hours after he had left a remote northern work camp. It was obvious to everyone involved in finding and recovering his remains that Kenton had been killed and partially eaten by wolves.

Prior to Kenton, there was no record of any human being killed by wild wolves in North America. Captive wolves had killed humans, but never wild wolves. Farley Mowat had written *Never Cry Wolf*, a book that drove that point home. It turns out that Mowat made up most of what he wrote, and *Never Cry Wolf* is more fiction than fact. But we can forgive him. He wasn't a scientist. His purpose was to sensationalize the wolf, and it worked. Public awareness of wolves increased. I read the book, and I too was fooled into believing it, even though I had grown up on a trapline and should have known better.

Over the past hundred years, wolves were almost exterminated from North America, mostly to accommodate cattle ranchers and on the insistence of big-game hunters. Sometimes governments were involved and paid bounties for wolves. Cattle ranchers and hunters are also voters. And, if you didn't know any better, it made sense to kill the wolves who attacked calves and competed with the hunters.

The death of Kenton Joel Carnegie occurred decades after any bounty had been paid for wolves. The wolf population had recovered and appeared healthy. Public support for wolves was high. There was no danger of public outrage against the wolf or renewed calls for its extermination. The incident provided the perfect opportunity to do some real science.

Because there was no record of a human having been killed by wild wolves in North America in over a century, the Saskatchewan coroner's office hired a wolf expert to investigate. The expert chosen was Paul Paquet from the University of Calgary. Paquet wrote a report, wherein he cast doubt on the initial investigation, manipulated the evidence, relied upon conjecture, and concluded that Kenton had been killed by a bear—even though bears would have been hibernating and no one had seen a bear or any evidence of a bear in the area at the time.

I was hired by Kenton's family to represent them at the coroner's inquest into his death. The coroner's jury saw through the biased report prepared by Paquet and concluded that the cause of Kenton's death was an attack by wolves.

Since Kenton's death and the coroner's inquest, no further investigation has occurred. No science has been done. We haven't studied wolves or the environment we share with them. It appears to me that the government's attitude is this: If we don't know, we don't have to do anything.

Truth is important.

If it had not been for Kim and Lori Carnegie's insistence that the truth be told about their son's death, this book would not have been written, and the coroner's inquest might have concluded differently. They demanded answers and refused to accept an obviously flawed report. By the time I was hired as their lawyer for the coroner's inquest, Kim and Lori had questioned the experts cited in the report and contacted other experts. My job was easy. They had done the hard work. All that was left for me was to present the evidence they had gathered that countered the findings in Paquet's report.

As we search for the truth, there are some things we will never know. What happened when Kenton first saw the wolves? Did his fight-or-flight instinct kick in? What happened when the wolves pulled him down the first time? What were his thoughts when he stood back up again?

He was young. He was bright. His whole future was in front of him. He was just beginning a career in geology. And all he did was go for a walk within sight of the camp, not far—he didn't intend to be gone long, just for a walk because the camp was too confining and his youth demanded that he be active.

What Kenton didn't know when he went for that walk in the afternoon of November 8, 2005, near the Points North camp was that there had been several wolf attacks on humans in that area over the previous twenty years. I was one of the people who had been attacked, and I personally know two others.

PART 1
EARLIER WOLF ENCOUNTERS

MY OWN ENCOUNTER

Having been born and raised in northern Saskatchewan, it was normal and natural that I should find myself working at a northern uranium mine as a young man. I was used to being outdoors in the natural environment, and I had seen a lot of things by the time I reached my late twenties. But a feeling I had when I was out walking near the mine site was like nothing I had felt before.

The hair on the back of my neck stood up. I turned and looked back the way I had come, to where the mine road curved around the hill. At first I didn't see him, until I looked closer. He was right behind me, crouched, belly down, ears laid back, his tail swishing.

It begins as a perfectly normal morning. I awake at a quarter to five, get out of bed, do a hundred push-ups, a hundred sit-ups, and a hundred leg lifts. Go down for breakfast in a normal mining camp, probably have bacon and eggs, fill a Thermos with coffee, and at about six o'clock begin walking the three kilometres from the mine camp to the mine shop.

I walk or run about a hundred kilometres per week: walk to the mine shop in the morning, run back to the camp at lunch, take the bus back to the mine shop after lunch, and run again after work. I don't jog. I'm doing the three kilometres in just over nine minutes. Then once or twice a week I run eight kilometres to the airport and back. Two or three times a week I use the weight room. Then there's cross-country skiing and snowshoeing. I am in the best shape of my life. Even better than when I completed Canadian Armed Forces basic training a decade earlier.

It is November 6, 1986. The moon is just past new and not visible. Sunrise is still a couple of hours away. There is snow, and a grader has left a windrow of hard pack and ice along the edge of the roadway.

"They can tell if you're afraid," my older brother Clifford had taught me when I was about six. "Don't run," my mother had warned. "If a dog comes after you, charge at it and yell." I grew up around sleigh dogs, in a community where sleigh dogs often ran loose and everyone knew that dogs can smell if you're afraid, and it makes them braver.

At no time do I feel afraid. My childhood training works. I won't allow myself that emotion. I do, however, mask it with anger. I learn that morning that anger is controllable. You can turn it on, and you can turn it up. I use it. I use anger not just to replace fear. I use it for energy.

I yell so loud that I spit out my dental plate that replaced a couple of front teeth I had lost in a fight, back when I was still fighting. I charge at him, as big and strong and mean as I can be, stomping my feet, arms up.

My bluff works. He turns and runs.

But not far.

Maybe six metres.

Turns and comes straight back.

I am by the edge of the road, by the windrow. Usually a dog will run if you raise an arm pretending you have a rock to throw. But this is no dog. He has never had a person throw rocks at him. Doesn't understand that gesture.

I need a real rock. All I can find in the windrow left by the grader is a hard chunk of snow. I meet his attack. A couple of stomping steps toward him as he comes. I throw and miss. He turns again.

And again goes only a short distance before he comes back.

Over and over and over and over.

I meet his attack with another chunk of snow, thrown and missed, feet stomping, yelling and cursing. I am ex-navy, a logger, and a miner. I have a large vocabulary of profanity that is part of my everyday language. But this morning the best I can come up with is to call him a "dirty black son-of-a-bitch."

He is black. Shiny black with flecks of silver on his sides. Today, thirty years later, I don't have to close my eyes to see him. He's healthy, strong, about a metre at the shoulder. He doesn't bark or growl or make any vocalization whatsoever. The only sound he makes is the click of his claws on the frozen roadway. I weigh seventy-eight kilos, and he weighs at least the same as I do, maybe even a bit more.

Sometimes when I go to get something to throw from the windrow, the chunk I grab is frozen down, and I have to struggle to get it loose, which means on these occasions when he comes back he gets even closer before I can meet his attack.

And fast.

The other thing that I remember clearly is how quickly he moves. At one point in our battle, I find a perfect throwing rock in the windrow, nice weight, and it fits into my hand.

"I am going to cave your fucken head in, you black son-of-a-bitch."

Maybe I shouldn't have told him what I was planning. I wait for him to come in close, within about sixty centimetres. I am in good shape. Strong, young. When I was still fighting, I had prided myself on the speed of my fists.

My throw is from shoulder height downward, with everything I have.

I miss.

He moves his head out of the way of the rock faster than I could believe was possible. Then turns and runs only to turn again and come back for more.

The road from the camp to the mine shop forks at about the halfway point, and one branch leads on the other side of the hill to the mill complex. A van comes from the mill and turns toward the camp. The driver doesn't see me, as I am partway around the hill toward the shop.

I decide to work my way back to the junction in case another vehicle comes by.

He comes at me. I meet him, stomping, swearing, and throwing. When he turns, I move a little way down the road and get my next throwing object. Eventually I make it to the junction.

There is a manhole there. A large galvanized metal culvert, about two metres in diameter, sticks up out of the ground sixty centimetres or so, closed at the top with a metal trap door over a ladder that leads down to some pipes and valves.

I take shelter in it. Climb partway down the ladder, my head and torso exposed.

He goes about four or five metres away and lies down. I imagine he intends to starve me out. We have a conversation wherein I exhibit my mastery of profanity. He doesn't respond, just lies there and waits.

At about six-thirty, the supervisor for the mill warehouse comes by, on his way to work a half-hour before crew change at seven.

I meet him on the road, speak to him through the open window. "Hey, buddy, how about giving me a ride to the mine shop? I got a wolf bothering me here."

"Sure thing."

"I'll just get you to shine your headlights here on the road. I spit out my false teeth and wouldn't mind finding them."

I find my teeth. Hear them snap when I step on them.

The wolf doesn't go anywhere. It won't come directly into the headlights, but it's circling, waiting.

Once I'm safely in the cab of the truck, the supervisor drives at him. The wolf runs up on a mound of dirt and stands there looking at us.

The only rifle on site is with the security guards. They are informed and go looking for the wolf. They never find it.

My anger stays with me for the rest of the day. When rumour comes that management is going to prohibit anyone from walking, it comes back full force. "No fucken way. They'll have to fire me first."

I need to walk. I need to walk at the end of that day, and the day following and the day after that, because I know that if I don't I might never be able to walk alone again.

For months and even years after, I force myself to walk, alone, in the dark, spinning around to look back at the slightest sound. Cameco, the mining corporation, would not allow anyone to carry a firearm on site, not even a pellet gun. I arm myself: a can of ether starting fluid with a Bic lighter taped on to it. It's clumsy. It requires two hands—one to hold down the valve on the spray can and the other to flick the lighter—but when the ether hits the spark it shoots a ball of flame about two metres. "Come on, you son-of-a-bitch, try me now."

It's more than just an uneasiness. Walking alone in the forest, my thoughts are constantly of wolves, what I am going to do, is there a tree large enough to climb? I am a writer, and long walks are a fundamental part of writing, when the mind puts together the pieces. It took a long time after the attack before I could walk alone and allow my mind to wander peacefully.

When Kenton Joel Carnegie was killed and partly consumed by wolves, his family hired me to represent them at the coroner's inquest. I was sent a large box of material as disclosure that included the police reports, Saskatchewan Environment and Resource Management (SERM) reports, and two photo booklets filled with pictures of the scene and of the autopsy. Those photographs were difficult to look at. Seeing what the wolves did to Kenton triggered me. It had been twenty years since my encounter with a wolf, but the anxiety and worry returned. I live two and a half kilometres from where I park my vehicle. It's a pleasant walk, and on a cold winter morning going in to work I am fully awake by the time I get to the truck. I started carrying a gun.

A decade after the coroner's inquest, when I started writing this book—going back through the files, looking at the photographs, interviewing the people who were there—I was triggered again. And again I experienced enough worry and anxiety on that walk in to and out from the cabin that I again began carrying a gun.

JIM DESROCHES'S STORY

"Wow! Am I ever lucky to see a wolf," was Jim Desroches's first thought.

He wasn't supposed to go over to the permanent camp. There were rules. He worked in the temporary camp made up of trailers pulled together over by the mill complex of the Key Lake uranium mine. But his girlfriend, Sandra, worked at the permanent camp.

The two camps operated under different assumptions. The temporary camp housed contractors, construction workers, tradespeople, and heavy equipment operators who were there to put the finishing touches on the recently built mill and open-pit uranium mine. The temporary camp had a seven-hundred-person licensed bar. The workers routinely brought bottles of alcohol with them and typically stayed in the camp on a three-weeks-at-work and one-week-at-home rotation. Alcohol was an accepted part of their lifestyle.

The permanent camp housed the employees of the Cameco Key Lake mine. It also had a bar. But its bar was only open for a few hours each evening and had a strict limit of two drinks per customer. Key Lake employees were not allowed to bring alcohol to work with them.

The rule Desroches disregarded was that people who worked in the temporary camp were not allowed to visit the permanent camp. The reason given for the rule was to limit the flow of alcohol from the temporary to the permanent camp. Cameco did not want the problems associated with the temporary construction workers' wild drinking habits to infect the full-time workers.

The only problem for Desroches was that Sandra had recently obtained full-time employment with the Key Lake mine and worked at the permanent camp. Desroches had been warned by his supervisor that he could be fired if he was caught sneaking over to visit her. He was also told that Cameco knew he was sneaking over and that they were watching.

He went anyway.

If anyone stopped him, he was just out for a jog in the evening. Not going anywhere, just up the road that direction. He would typically jog past the permanent camp, then take a left turn up the hill, and from this vantage watch to see where the security guards were on their rounds. When their truck was safely back at the gate house, he would slip down to visit Sandra.

On this cold night he had just begun jogging. He was nearing the junction where the road from the camp branched one way to the mine shop and the other toward the permanent camp.

The wolf had come over the hill from the direction of the mine shop and onto the road. It ran parallel to Desroches on the opposite side for a while. This was when Desroches thought about how lucky he was. He could distinctly hear the sound of the wolf's claws clicking on the frozen roadway.

Then the wolf turned and came straight across the road toward him. Desroches still wasn't afraid—more in awe of the large black and grey animal right in front of him. Then the wolf lunged, going for his throat. He swung his arm in the way. It grabbed the back of the sleeve of his parka between his elbow and his shoulder. The wolf's jaws were mere inches from his face just before it latched on. Desroches's memory of the teeth, still clear thirty years later when I interviewed him, was that "they were as long as cigarettes."

Then the fear kicked in. He had an image in his mind of the wolf shaking him to death.

Desroches described it as near panic, with him screaming and shouting "Get the fuck away from me" and punching with everything he had over his left elbow with his right fist and connecting with the wolf's snout. The punch convinced the wolf to let go of Desroches's parka sleeve but not before tearing a large hole in it. Later, when a nurse examined the arm, it was purple from elbow to shoulder. The big parka over a heavy sweater and bulky winter clothing saved him. The wolf's teeth did break the skin, but the injury was minor.

The wolf had been dislodged by a punch to the nose, but it wasn't finished. It lunged again and again at Desroches, but these lunges did not have the ferocity of the initial attack. To Desroches it seemed that the wolf was testing him. He knew enough not to turn his back and run. He backed up, swearing and yelling, and when the wolf lunged at his face he batted away at it with both hands in big black leather mitts. He kept backing up, swearing and screaming, but he kept facing the attack and fighting back, lunge after lunge after lunge.

Then the wolf stopped.

Just stopped. Stood in the middle of the road and turned its head, listening.

Desroches kept backing away, and when he thought he was far enough, he finally turned and ran. A moment later he heard a vehicle approach. The wolf had apparently heard it first. By the time the truck arrived, the wolf was gone. The only remaining evidence was Desroches's and the wolf's tracks in the snow and Desroches's torn parka.

In an interview with Desroches in 2017, his memory of the attack was meticulous. He was able to remember exact details of what had occurred thirty-three years earlier, even though it was something that he rarely spoke about. After the attack, he had told people about it. The problem was that most people didn't believe him. Rather than risk being accused of lying or exaggerating, Desroches simply quit talking about it.

FRED DESJARLAIS'S ENCOUNTER

It was New Year's Eve, 2004, when Fred Desjarlais met the wolf that would change him. In 2005, the year that followed, there would be more wolf attacks in northern Saskatchewan.

Desjarlais said that when he left the mine shop that evening, he thought about carrying a stick.

I asked him if that thought might have been intuitive, considering what was about to happen. He said no, it was just a thought he'd had as he left on his way to camp at the end of his shift.

Desjarlais had a walk/run routine of leaving the mine shop at a run, slowing to a walk at the first intersection, then running to the next, and then walking again. He had finished the first run portion and started to walk when he heard a sound behind him that might have been a growl. He turned, and the wolf lunged for his throat. He described the encounter in terms of pure adrenalin, strength, speed, and energy.

He managed to get the wolf into a headlock, but in his attempt to throw it to the ground the wolf came loose and got its teeth into the back of Desjarlais's right arm and into his side.

Desjarlais had left the mine shop about five minutes prior to the official end of his shift at 7:00 p.m. The sun had set more than two hours earlier. He was near the junction where one road led to the mill complex and the other led to the mine camp, the same junction as in Desroches's story and mine. The road here was wide—twenty-eight feet across—and this fight was taking place near its centre.

Desjarlais jumped back onto his feet in time to meet the next lunge. He got his arm up, and the wolf placed both of its paws on Desjarlais's horizontal forearm. Desjarlais recalls a distinct moment when he looked beyond his arm into the wolf's face, not more than a couple feet from his own. He has a clear memory of the image, of looking into the wolf's eyes. It is an image that still haunts him.

He shoved it away, and it dropped to all fours only to lunge again. This time it grabbed Desjarlais by the hip. His memory of the bite, of the teeth penetrating his skin, was that it felt like fire, like red-hot iron.

He dropped down on top of the wolf and grabbed it again around the neck with both arms. He was facing toward its tail, its snout pointed toward his stomach. He held the wolf down. Desjarlais is a large man, solid and well built. He used his weight and his strength to hold it down. He could feel the wolf's windpipe against his forearm.

Later his chest would hurt from putting all his weight on top of the wolf's head.

Suddenly the wolf went still. It wasn't fighting anymore.

I am surmising here based on my experience with sleigh dogs. The remainder of this paragraph is pure conjecture. I now have eleven sleigh dogs and have had as many as twenty-six at one time. Most of my dogs are Siberian husky. Some of them are part wolf. Some are a quarter, some an eighth, and most are a sixteenth wolf. Discipline is required to maintain order with a dog team. I find the most successful way to discipline a rowdy dog is to grab it by the throat and put it down to the snow standing over it in a dominating posture. The pure Siberian husky dogs usually squirm a little and eventually get it that they are not in charge. Dogs that are part wolf, however, are more likely to lie perfectly still in a position of submission. It seems they see me as the alpha male of their pack, and they conform to their pack rules. I suspect this is what happened when Desjarlais's forearm was across the wolf's windpipe. It instinctively went into a posture of submission.

The bus that carries the miners from the mine shop to the mine camp at the end of the shift has two metal wheel chocks that rest on steel pins welded to the front bumper. It would have left the mine shop at precisely five minutes after seven.

Desjarlais heard the bus coming. He could hear the wheel chocks rattling.

The driver would later tell Desjarlais that he had no intention of stopping because he was not sure what he was seeing on the roadway—a wolf and something else. It wasn't until they were close and the headlights showed Desjarlais as well that he decided to stop, and the bus skidded to within a few metres of Desjarlais and the wolf. The miners, in their rush to get off the bus to assist, jammed up the entrance, pushing against a door that opened inward.

Desjarlais made it onto the bus, and the wolf got away.

The nurse at the mine camp put ten stitches into Desjarlais's hip where the wolf had torn him. He was then evacuated by airplane to a hospital in Saskatoon. But it was New Year's Eve, and the emergency ward was filled with drunks with broken hands and smashed faces and various injuries from drunken brawling or falling. Desjarlais waited for three hours without seeing a physician and then went home. He returned in the morning and was administered twenty-six rabies shots: ten into the wounds, fifteen around them, and one for good measure. He then went back to the hospital once a week for additional shots.

The next morning Key Lake staff shot two wolves. The first one was near where the attack on Desjarlais had occurred. Another wolf was shot near the open-pit mine. This second wolf was not afraid when approached and did not leave when attempts were made to scare it off.

Key Lake staff had verbal permission from SERM to destroy wolves because of the attack on Desjarlais and would later receive formal permission in the form of wildlife nuisance permits. Both wolves were sent to the Western College of Veterinary Medicine at the University of Saskatchewan for necropsies, which were performed by Dr. Gary Wobeser on January 5, 2005.

The wolf identified as DO5-186 was an adult female. She had at least four placenta scars on her uterus, indicating that she had had pups in the past. Blood found in both of her frontal sinuses was assumed to have been the result of the gunshot wound.

Her outer right maxillary incisor was broken. Incisors are the front teeth that animals use for biting and are between the long canine teeth. This broken tooth was in her top jaw. The opposing incisor on her bottom jaw had a broken tip. All of the remaining lower incisor teeth showed some wear. The canine teeth and molars were normal. Her age wasn't determined, but the wear on her teeth and the fact that she'd had pups indicated that she was not young.

She also had a problem with her left foreleg. It could not be extended fully at the carpal or wrist joint, indicating either an injury or a birth defect that might have caused a slight limp.

The autopsy did show some subcutaneous fat—the fat that is normally found just under the skin of animals. But the amount found was minimal: less than a centimetre over the loin area. The intestines contained normal amounts of fat. The bone marrow was pink and firm. She was a little thin, but she was not starving. If she had been starving, the intestinal fat would have been less, and the bone marrow would have begun to discolour.

The report states, "No gross or microscopic lesions were identified that would explain aggressive behaviour. There was no evidence of infectious disease and the brain tissue tested negative for rabies."

The other wolf shot at the Key Lake site and sent for testing was a younger adult female in excellent body condition. This wolf had approximately 2.4 centimetres of fat over the loin area and abundant internal fat.

The brains of both wolves were sent to Lethbridge, Alberta, for rabies testing. The results were negative: neither wolf had rabies.

Delmar Wolkowsky was an environment technician for Cameco, the operator of the Key Lake uranium mine. He visited the scene at about two o'clock the next afternoon, or about nineteen hours after the attack on Desjarlais. That morning at about ten a wolf was shot near where Desjarlais and the wolf had had their encounter, which was about three hundred metres from the main camp. Wolkowsky was looking for evidence that might link the wolf that was shot with the one that had bitten Desjarlais. Had they killed the correct wolf?

A light, transparent layer of snow had fallen, but the site was still very visible. Wolkowsky wrote in his report that "there were human tracks and wolf tracks and signs that a struggle had taken place. There was no evidence that any other human or animal had visited the scene since the attack. Had there been another visitor other than myself, it would have been obvious."

In clean, uncontaminated snow, he found a row of brown droplets in a curved line about twelve inches (30.5 cm) long. There were ten droplets about an inch (2.5 cm) apart and sixteen inches (40.6 cm) away from the nearest disturbed area. The droplets appeared to have been flung there. Wolkowsky was certain that these droplets were bodily fluids from either the wolf or Desjarlais because they could not have come from any other source. He suspected they were fecal matter but not firm droppings. He gathered the frozen droplets and placed them in a plastic bag, wrote his initials and the time and date on the bag, and placed the bag in the freezer of Cameco's Environment Department.

Dr. Yves Plante of Bova-Can Laboratories in Saskatoon tested the sample against tissue from the wolf using DNA analysis. His February 8, 2005, report concludes as follows: "In my opinion, the bodily fluid collected at the attack site comes from the animal identified as DO5-186." Plante estimated the probability that the two samples came from two different animals at less than one chance in two billion.

The wolf that attacked Desjarlais was the same wolf that was shot near where the encounter occurred. This wolf was thin but not starving. She had slight damage to her teeth and a problem with her left front wrist. She was not sick and did not have rabies.

As a result of the wolf attack on Desjarlais, Cameco made changes to the garbage dump at its Key Lake mine. A sturdy electric fence was installed. Wolkowsky and the other environmental technicians on site were required to inspect the fence and the dump twice a day: specifically, to go there, open the gate, make sure the electricity was on, drive down into the dump, and check for wolves or bears. Wolkowsky told me that he never saw a wolf or a bear in the dump after the fence was installed. He did see lots of ravens, and seagulls and bald eagles taking a free meal, and even occasionally a fox, but never any large animals. He retired from the Key Lake mine in 2012.

Desjarlais's encounter with the wolf had long-lasting impacts on him. He became terrified of being out at night. He can no longer work night shifts. When I spoke to him twelve years after the incident, he still struggled with his emotions when he recounted certain parts of the fight, espe-cially the part where the wolf's paws were on his forearm and he looked straight across into her face. His experience that evening altered his life. The trauma of the attack and the bites continues to affect him.

I've known Fred Desjarlais for over thirty years. He was working at the Key Lake mine when I was hired on by the company, and he is still there. The Fred I remembered I would describe as strong, peaceful, and capable. The Fred I interviewed a dozen years after his being attacked by a wolf was still strong, peaceful, and capable, but he had obviously been seriously wounded. He had lost a big chunk of his confidence.

TODD SVARCKOPF AND CHRIS VAN GALDER

Ten months after the attack on Desjarlais, just 145 kilometres away, planes were avoiding a big part of northern Saskatchewan because of bad weather. Low clouds meant that the visibility necessary for flying was too poor to work safely. If you can't see where you're going, it's difficult to find the airport when it's time to land. No plane meant no work for Todd Svarckopf and Chris Van Galder. Tired of playing soccer in an empty hangar, they went for a walk around noon. It was November 4, 2005.

Both men worked for Sander Geophysics. Their jobs involved the creation of high-resolution airborne surveys, using fixed-wing aircraft. On this job, they were using a Cessna Grand Caravan, a single-engine turboprop plane that in normal use would carry nine passengers. When used for geophysics, the plane is outfitted with instruments that measure gravity, magnetism, and radiation. The plane flies over an area following a precise grid. The instruments record data that are then put together in a map. The surveys are prepared for mining companies looking for minerals in the area.

Svarckopf had been on this job for three months. During that time he had been away from the camp by himself numerous times fishing and had never encountered a wolf.

The camp at Points North Landing encompassed an airstrip, a twelve-thousand-square-foot hangar, workshops, warehouses, and accommodations. In the 1980s when the camp began, Points North was the end of the road. Mining and exploration of the Athabasca Basin were booming. Located in northern Saskatchewan, the Athabasca Basin is primarily sand with a rolling topography sparsely covered by pine forest. Around the edges of the basin were the Key Lake mine at the southern edge, the Cluff Lake mine toward the west, and the Rabbit Lake mine toward the northeast. McArthur River, McLean Lake, and Cigar Lake mines would open later. They all mine uranium.

Points North catered to the mining and exploration industries by providing camp services, transportation, and freight. A company like Sander Geophysics could work in this remote region without having to build its own airstrip and camp. I've stayed at Points North. The food is good, the camp is clean, the accommodations are comfortable. This is a work camp. There is no entertainment.

A person can go a little stir-crazy in camp if there is no work to keep him occupied. In an interview with Corporal Marion of the Royal Canadian Mounted Police, Svarckopf said that weather complications with their aircraft had grounded them for several weeks, and he had just learned that the plane would not be flying that day either.

Svarckopf and Van Galder decided to go to an old junkyard on the opposite side of the airstrip from the camp to look at several old discarded airplanes. They crossed the airstrip at about its midpoint and entered a forested area that was mostly swampy without much for tree cover. Here they encountered the first wolf. They spotted this grey-coloured wolf about two hundred metres from them toward the northeast. When the wolf came toward them, they began to back out of the area. The wolf came right up to Svarckopf.

Van Galder asked, "What should we do?"

Svarckopf replied, "Whatever we do, we don't turn and run."

Svarckopf yelled at it, and the wolf retreated a few steps. He and Van Galder continued to back out of the wooded area. They weren't very far in, only a few hundred metres; by looking over his shoulder, Svarckopf could see the camp behind him.

The grey wolf kept getting closer and closer, becoming less and less afraid. At that point another wolf showed up, a white one. Now the grey wolf didn't seem afraid at all and became more aggressive, approaching Van Galder, the smaller of the two men. Van Galder yelled at it, but this time it didn't retreat.

Svarckopf was focusing on the white wolf. Van Galder yelled for him, and Svarckopf turned his back toward the white wolf—it came even closer while his back was turned. Svarckopf turned back to the white wolf and was able to scare it away a short distance.

At this point, Svarckopf worked his way over toward Van Galder, who was being confronted by the grey wolf. This wolf was down on its haunches very close to Van Galder. Svarckopf had picked up a stick on his way over and gave it to Van Galder. With Van Galder at his back, Svarckopf said, they were able to keep an eye on both wolves. It seemed to him that the wolves were trying to separate the two men. With both of them carrying sticks and watching each other's back, they worked their way to the edge of the airstrip. The wolves positioned themselves between the men and the camp, seemingly, to Svarckopf, to keep them in the wooded area.

The pair of wolves stayed with the two men as they crossed the airstrip and did not stop acting aggressively until the men were nearly inside the camp compound. Svarckopf said the whole encounter probably lasted not more than ten to fifteen minutes, but it felt like a lifetime. During this time, the wolves did not make any vocalizations. They did not growl or bark or howl.

Toward the end of the encounter, Van Galder took four photographs of the wolves. Both men knew that without photographs no one was likely to believe them.

Referring to the wolf shown in Figure 2, Edward Kowal, wildlife program manager and provincial elk manager, Resource Stewardship Branch of SERM, stated in an email

Figure 2. Todd Svarckopf confronting a wolf near the site of the Kenton Carnegie attack. (Photograph courtesy of Coroner's Office, Government of Saskatchewan.)

to fellow resource officers, "In looking at the snarling wolf, I noticed that it is probably a dominant wolf (tail wagging, etc.) with a second wolf looking on. As I looked at these aggressive gestures and posturing by the wolf in such close proximity to the geologist, and given the circumstances of habituation to humans at the camp, I'm thinking that 'you're a dead man!'"

DEATH BY WOLF: KENTON CARNEGIE'S STORY

KENTON GOES MISSING

On November 8, 2005, just three days after the attack on Todd
Svarckopf and Chris Van Galder, the weather was still bad.
The planes were still not flying, and the camp at Points North
would have felt small. Kenton Joel Carnegie asked Van Galder
to accompany him on a walk. Van Galder declined. He warned
Kenton that there were wolves out there and that he should not
go. Kenton went anyway. He said he wasn't going far, that he
was just going around the lakeshore and would be back by 5:00
p.m. This was at about 3:30 p.m. Van Galder would later tell
Constable Alphonse Noey of the Wollaston Lake detachment of
the Royal Canadian Mounted Police, "He was fine. He wanted
ah...to go for a walk. I think he was feeling a little stir crazy."

Kenton had been at the Points North camp for only about
two weeks. He was a third-year geological engineering co-op
student from the University of Waterloo. The co-op program
required that students, beginning in the second year, alter-
nate four months of studying with four months of actual
hands-on work. Luise Sander for Sander Geophysics said that
her company preferred to work with Waterloo because, in her
experience, that university had "good students and a long,
successful track record with the co-op program."

Kenton was one of the top students at Waterloo. He had
an A grade average. Outgoing, he hosted a rock radio show

on campus. He was known to be artistic and, as is common among artistic people, he was gifted in mathematics. Despite being outgoing and energetic, Kenton was not known to be a risk taker.

But who was he?

Friends described him as a talented "free spirit." He was an artist. He had a large collection of classical art on his computer. His sketches of natural landscapes were well known among his family and friends. Some were on display at his funeral.

"He wasn't a typical kind of engineer," said Nick Lawler, friend and president of the University of Waterloo Engineering Society. "He was very into art. Most of us are into math."

But math was one of Kenton's best subjects.

Leo Rothenburg, one of Kenton's professors and chair of the University of Waterloo's civil engineering department, thought Kenton's work would have been a dream job—working in a remote place, surrounded by nature. Rothenburg noted that "he was a very kind soul, always trying to help everyone. He was also a very good artist. He does sketching, and maybe that's why he was walking in the woods, trying to find a place where he could sit down and sketch."

There were rumours at the time that Kenton had gone out to sketch wolves. He had not. He did not have either a sketch pad or pencils with him.

His artistic interests also included music. While Kenton was a student at Waterloo, his radio show on CKMS FM, called *Strange Brew*, featured rare classic rock, psychedelic rock, and folk music. He had emailed Kate George, program coordinator at CKMS, to lobby for a wintertime slot: "At the moment I'm living in Points North, Saskatchewan (way up north in a mining camp) and a few weeks ago I was livin' in Iqaluit, Nunavut.

Both places, I've still managed to listen to CKMS online (even calling in to my buddy Psychedelic Pete's show)."

Pete Ahrens, otherwise known as Psychedelic Pete, was Kenton's radio mentor. I interviewed Ahrens in late September 2018. He is an old hippie (his words) and was in his mid-fifties when he began to mentor Kenton. His memory was that he first met Kenton when Kenton was outside the radio studio looking through the window. Ahrens invited him in. Kenton wanted to know about the rare 1960s underground, soul, psychedelic, and garage music Ahrens played.

Ahrens's impression was that Kenton was very bright and capable, that he was good at anything he did. But more than that, Kenton had an aura around him of peace, something special. He was friendly and easy to be with, "a great kid," who could have gone on to do anything he wanted. Ahrens said that Kenton looked kind of like Cat Stevens—maybe it was his aura of peace that gave that impression.

Ahrens didn't know much about what happened to Kenton. Thirteen years after the investigation and a coroner's inquest, he believed that Kenton had gone out that day to sketch. Rumours have a way of propagating and perpetuating themselves.

Kenton was also a scientist. He was studying geology. Ahrens described him as a genius combination of artsy and engineer. According to his professor Rothenburg, "He always grasped concepts probably much faster than anyone I came across."

We will never know why Kenton went for a walk that afternoon. But we can understand why a young, intelligent, free-spirited artist would feel confined in a remote camp after a long period without work to occupy his mind.

Meals at Points North are served cafeteria style in the camp's dining room. The Sander Geophysics crew, comprising

Kenton, Van Galder, Svarckopf, and Christy Oysteryk, usually ate together. On November 8, 2005, Kenton didn't show up for supper at six o'clock.

Van Galder went looking for him. He first checked Kenton's room, thinking he might be watching a Leafs game, because Kenton had said that he intended to. He wasn't there. Van Galder then checked around camp. He didn't find Kenton anywhere.

He then told Svarckopf of his unsuccessful search, and together, at about six-thirty, they went to Mark Eikel, the camp manager, for assistance and a truck to go looking for Kenton. Using the truck and following the road around the shore, the three of them were able to see human tracks in the fresh snow. The tracks followed the shore, occasionally going down to the frozen lake, on the ice, and then back up on the bank again. They also saw several wolf tracks.

Svarckopf climbed into the back of the truck and rode there in the hope that he could see better and maybe hear something. When the road they were travelling on diverged from the path along the shore, all three men got out. They saw human tracks leading up a trail that went to a cabin farther along the shore. Here they saw more wolf tracks.

They decided to go back to camp and get a rifle.

Once they had the rifle they drove back around the lake to the cabin. Eikel hoped that if something had happened, Kenton would have taken shelter there. No fresh tracks were visible at the cabin, so they returned to where the trail and road diverged—the last place they had seen Kenton's tracks. They followed the trail in using flashlights. Sunrise this time of year is at about eight-thirty and sunset a few minutes before five. By the time the men got to the place where the trail diverged, at about seven, on a night that was overcast with the moon only in its first quarter, it was quite dark. Eikel was in the lead with Svarckopf and Van Galder following. They came to a spot where there had clearly been a disturbance; it involved multiple wolf tracks.

Farther on up the trail, Eikel noted that the human footprints he'd been following now travelled in both directions, away from him and toward him. He realized that Kenton must have turned back. The three men turned around and returned the way they had come. Now Svarckopf and Van Galder were leading with Eikel in the rear. When they got to the spot of the disturbance noted earlier, Eikel panned his flashlight off the trail down toward a lower muskeg area.

He wasn't a hundred percent sure of what he was seeing. He said to Svarckopf and Van Galder, "Okay, you guys, let's... let's go. This isn't good."

Eikel didn't want to see it. He was uncertain of how he would react if he saw it. He was also uncertain of how Svarckopf and Van Galder would react.

They returned to the Points North camp and phoned the RCMP.

But what if Kenton was still alive?

Eikel was second-guessing himself.

What did he really see out there?

He talked it over with Robert (Bob) Burseth, an employee of Points North. They decided to go back out, each with a rifle.

At 2:42 p.m. the next afternoon, Eikel gave a statement to Constable Noey of the RCMP. He was still obviously upset.

I saw Bob, discussed it with him. Ah...and then I started second guessing myself a little bit, like maybe I didn't see what I thought I saw and then I was concerned that maybe he was...he was still alive so ahm...I said to Bob, "Let's go back out there." So Bob yeah, Bob had a rifle, I had my rifle. We went back out there ah...to the spot he was...like we stayed up top. We didn't walk down to him, ahm...we just...just had the flashlight and ah...just looked I guess, at him, like I mean, it was...it was quite...like he wasn't alive... like it just...I mean, like I just, you know...ah...and we came back...like I don't...I don't really...if we were there...like we weren't there for very long, I don't think. We came back and ahm...I may have phoned you guys again. I don't even really remember, then we kind of felt like we should be over there, like on the road....Just to kind of...I don't know what it is but I...you just feel uneasy about somebody... being out there, ah...so we kind of went and sat there for a while, just around the corner.

Later in his statement to Constable Noey, Eikel tried to describe what he saw when he and Burseth returned to see if Kenton was still alive:

Not when I first saw him and like when Bob and I went back, ahm...like I can't even really remem—...I just... like I remember seeing his...his...head and I remember I think...like, and I don't...like I don't know how...but for some reason, I remember thinking his eyes were open or something, like and I was sho—...like I was trying to fig- ure out if he was breathing or something without actually having to walk up there like, 'cause I couldn't do it. But I saw behind him, like parts of his body that were eaten, like legs or ar—...like it was ahm...what I saw didn't to me and like I said, it could be a person's mind but it didn't...what I saw didn't seem, you know, you picture a human being or whatever, it wasn't things...I didn't...it just wasn't right, like there was and ah...but there was...there was just...like there was...like it was.'

Burseth and Eikel waited in the truck parked on the road near where the body was last seen and awaited the arrival of the police.

ROBERT BURSETH'S STORY

In 2005 Robert Burseth had worked at the Points North camp for about seventeen years. He was very familiar with the North. His wife, Rosalie Tsannie-Burseth, lived at Wollaston Lake and was, among other things, the coroner for the region.

Burseth was in the office on November 8, 2005, at about 6:30 p.m., when he was contacted by Eikel, the camp manager. Eikel asked Burseth if he had heard what happened. Burseth hadn't. Eikel told him, "One of the Sander crew went walking at about three o'clock, was supposed to be back at five and ah...wasn't back yet."

Eikel was getting flashlight batteries and preparing to go look for the missing crew member. Burseth watched Eikel and two members of the Sander crew leave in a truck and head south along the lake. There are so many lakes in this part of northern Saskatchewan that, despite this one being 2.4 kilometres long and 1 kilometre wide, it doesn't officially, or even unofficially, have a name. People simply refer to it as "the lake."

Burseth could see the lights of the truck as it drove in at a cabin on the south shore across from the camp. He was working in the shop a few minutes later when he received a call on the radio from Eikel informing him that they had "some troubles." Despite the brevity of the communication, Burseth knew something serious had happened. He phoned Rosalie in Wollaston because she was the coroner, and he assumed she would contact the police. Eikel and the other two crew members returned and told him that they had found the body.

Burseth worked a rotation of two weeks at work followed by two weeks at home. He didn't know Kenton. Kenton had come into camp on the same day that Burseth had gone out on his rotation two weeks earlier.

All three of the returning men were shaken up by what they had discovered. Eikel seemed especially unnerved. He asked Burseth to accompany him back out there. The two men each took a rifle and went back. The body was in the same place where Eikel had found it earlier. Both men stayed up on the bank and did not walk down to where the body was located, in the lower muskeg area. They stayed only a few minutes at the scene—just long enough to determine for sure that Kenton wasn't still alive.

They returned to the camp, and Eikel continued to try contacting the RCMP. The Wollaston Lake detachment has only a few members, and after 5:00 p.m. there would likely have been just one or two officers on duty. If they were out on a call, there wouldn't be anyone in the office to answer the phone. In situations like this the phone automatically reroutes to a dispatcher in Regina who takes the call and then attempts to contact the officers by radio if the situation is urgent.

After the RCMP were successfully contacted, Eikel and Burseth went back out for no other reason than there was a human being out there, and the body should not be left alone. They stayed in their truck and did not go back to the body but just stayed nearby on the road and waited for the police to arrive.

In an interview in 2017 Burseth readily admitted that he was not an expert when it came to tracking, but he could tell the difference between a wolf and a bear track. The bear track is of a different shape and is usually quite a bit larger than a wolf track. Burseth remembered that a few days following the incident with Kenton a worker at Points North returned from taking garbage out to the dump. This worker reported that wolves had come right up to the loader he was operating. Burseth took a rifle and rode on the back of the loader out to the dump. Four wolves were there. He shot one, and it ran off to the side. He shot another one that died right away. When he went to check on the first one he'd shot, he found it dead a short distance from where he had first seen it.

To Burseth, this was simply a job that needed to be done. Someone had to do it. He was there, and he was able. He has since killed more wolves at Points North. During our interview he said that the last wolf he shot was about three years ago. It had come into camp, was hanging around the kitchen and behaving unafraid.

He has seen other wolves occasionally over the past almost thirty years at Points North. They are attracted to the garbage dump. But they are not a common sight. They are usually only seen in the distance and flee if approached. That sort of wolf he has no problem with. If a wolf or two passes near camp, crosses the lake, or heads down the road, he leaves them to their business.

The garbage dump now has a fence around it, but wolves and even bears dig under it, drawn by the promise of a free meal.

Burseth's experience in November 2005 did not have a major impact on him. He said that it made him think when he was in the woods to be more careful and aware of his surroundings.

WHAT CONSTABLE NOEY SAW

Constable Alphonse Noey of the Wollaston Lake RCMP detachment received a call at about 7:00 p.m. on November 8, 2005, advising him that a body had been found near the Points North camp. Wollaston Lake does not have road access. There is an ice road that crosses the lake most winters, but the lake is so large it usually doesn't freeze over until late December. Noey had to charter a plane from Transwest Air to get to Points North, sixty-five kilometres to the northwest.

He and Tsannie-Burseth, the coroner, arrived at Points North at 9:35 p.m. He spoke with Van Galder, Svarckopf, Burseth, and Eikel and then went to the scene.

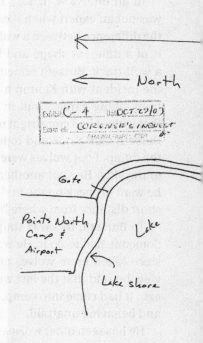

Figure 3. RCMP Constable Alphonse Noey's hand-drawn map of the death scene. (Photograph courtesy of Coroner's Office, Government of Saskatchewan.)

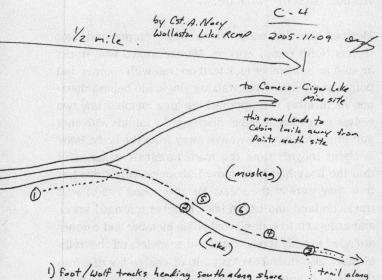

by Cst. A. Noey
Wollaston Lake RCMP

C-4

2005-11-09

½ mile.

to Cameco - Cigar Lake
Mine site

this road leads to
Cabin 1mile away from
Points north site

(muskag)

(Lake)

trail along
shore
to Cabin

1) foot/Wolf tracks heading south along shore

2) foot tracks along trail. Lots of Wolf tracks in snow.
this is were 1st search team turned around to
get rifle due to wolf tracks.

3) furthest foot prints went. Stood at shore line before heading
back. May have tried to get attention from Points north
camp as it is a clear line of site. Wolf tracks Coming
from south trail & Lake ice.

4) Snow is disturbed. Looks like someone rolling in snow.
Someone or something. 1st attack.

5) Ran to this point. Half on trail & half in muskag. Lots of
disturbance in snow. Lots of blood. One area showed
blood drops. May have stood there bleeding. Kill site.
this is where 1st search party saw body (Eikel).

6) When Cst. Noey arrived. Location of body. Moved 20 meters.
Member had to shoot shotgun in air to scare 2 wolves
away from body/scene.

His notes describe what he saw:

Member attended scene along with coroner and PNC [Points North camp] workers. Member noted wolf tracks around area. Member took lead on trail with coroner and points north employees walking single file behind member. As member was approaching area member saw two wolves near body. Member discharged 2 rounds with shot gun in the air to scare wolves away from the body. Body is about 100yrds from the road. BURSETH commented that the body had been moved about 50 yrds since last time they were at the scene. Member noted lots of wolf tracks on land and frozen lake. Member informed EIKEL and BURSETH to wait on trail while member and coroner attended to body (body was about 20 meters off the trail). Member also instructed EIKEL to discharge his rifle into the air as member can hear wolves in the forest around body. BURSETH advised member if a fire is made on the trail that would help keep wolves away from area. Member and coroner attend to body. Member took pictures of area and body. At scene about 40–45 mi.

He took thirty photographs of the scene that night.

The next day Noey flew back to Points North to examine the area in daylight and take more pictures. He took forty-six photographs before the camera's battery died. He also made a map (Figure 3) that indicates his interpretation of the tracks.

Kenton had left Points North camp heading southward along the shoreline. He had followed a path that ran on higher ground between the lake and the muskeg inland. These minor geological formations are common around lakes that freeze over. Ice expands over the winter because of extreme

Figure 4. Wolf tracks near the site of the Kenton Carnegie attack. (Photograph courtesy of Coroner's Office, Government of Saskatchewan.)

Figure 5. Disturbed snow at the site of the initial attack on Kenton Carnegie. (Photograph courtesy of Coroner's Office, Government of Saskatchewan.)

cold and pushes material up onto the shore. Over geological time, these ridges can become quite pronounced.

Kenton's tracks went to a spot about a kilometre away from the Points North camp, where he had apparently stood on the shore and had a clear view across the lake toward the camp. At this point Noey noted the tracks of two wolves on the ice coming from the west across the lake toward where Kenton had been standing (Figure 4).

Kenton's tracks turned back at this point, marked as 3 on the map. Noey noted that at the position marked as 4, the snow had been disturbed by what looked like someone rolling in the snow (Figure 5). He interpreted these tracks as the spot where the wolves first brought Kenton down.

Noey then followed Kenton's tracks northward, noting that some of the tracks were on the trail and some in the muskeg area adjacent to the trail. He found a spot where the tracks

Figure 6. Bloodstained snow where Kenton Carnegie's body was found. (Photograph courtesy of Coroner's Office, Government of Saskatchewan.)

indicated that Kenton had stood for a moment, and there were drops of blood on the snow. Point 5 on the map corresponds to several of the photographs taken by Noey. This is the kill site where Eikel, Van Galder, and Svarckopf first spotted the body.

Point 6 on Noey's map indicates the spot where the constable found Kenton's body—and where two wolves were feeding on it and where he fired two shotgun blasts into the air to scare the wolves away.

When I started writing this book, I quickly realized that I should interview Noey.

But where was he? RCMP officers are moved frequently from one detachment to another, with a typical stay of less than five years. Noey could be anywhere by now. Maybe I could get one of my officer friends to check for me. But I didn't need to. Within a couple of days of my thinking I needed to contact him, Noey contacted me on Facebook about my book *Firewater: How Alcohol Is Killing My People (and Yours)*.

I interviewed him in Melfort, Saskatchewan—his latest posting—on February 3, 2018. Born in 1967, Noey described his earliest years on the reserve at Fond du Lac as a beautiful time. His father was a hunter and fisher, and they had a good home in a good community where he had relatives: grandparents, aunts and uncles, cousins. Fond du Lac, in his memory, was a place where respect for Elders was fundamental to community cohesion. Alcohol was a rarity. There were no police. Other than the word of the Elders, the only enforcement of rules was done by Louis Mercredi Sr., who patrolled the community with a long willow switch and sent home any children that he caught out at night later than they needed to be.

Noey remembered moving to Uranium City in the 1970s. His family crossed Lake Athabasca in a freighter canoe, and the big lake had been rough. Bobby Auger gave them a ride from the lake into Uranium City, where they stayed in a friend's basement suite until Noey's dad found them a place of their own.

Uranium City was where alcohol became a significant factor in his family. He recalled as a child becoming anxious days before payday—a feeling he described as "a sinking feeling in your tummy"—because he anticipated the partying and the violence.

His father bought him a snow machine. The first one was an Elan, then a 250 Ski-Doo Citation. I remember these fast, light little machines that were noted for beating machines with engines much larger than their meagre 250cc. The memory that Noey wanted to share wasn't about racing, though; it was about trying to run over wolves with his machine out on the lake and how after his investigation of Kenton Carnegie's death that memory kept returning—especially of the one wolf that turned back and lunged at him.

His family left Uranium City in 1983, when Noey was sixteen, so when he was out chasing wolves he would have been a young teen thinking what he was doing was all fun and excitement. They moved to Prince Albert so that he and his siblings could get a good education. When Noey's youngest sister graduated from Grade 12, his parents moved back to Fond du Lac, where his father has since reconnected to the land and hunting and fishing.

Like many northerners, Noey ended up in the mines. He worked at Rabbit Lake for seven years as a surveyor. There he met my younger brother Stanley. Northern Saskatchewan, despite its large geography, is a place where you don't have to talk to someone for very long before you find connections to other people you both know or, more likely, are related to.

Noey had always wanted to be a police officer. But the Dene People refer to the police as "Denenaltsi Dene," the ones who take people away. His grandmother was very opposed to his joining the RCMP, until he explained to her that he wasn't joining to be a bully. He wanted to help people not go to jail. Even his wife hoped that he would fail at some point during the enlistment and training process.

Wollaston Lake was one of Noey's earliest postings as an RCMP officer. He chose it because he didn't have any relatives there. But people move around. He said the hardest thing he's had to do as a police officer was to arrest his cousin for being drunk and disorderly. His cousin said, "Just do it. It's your job."

The other part of his career that Noey wanted to talk about were the nightmares.

He kept seeing Kenton running from the wolves, the wolves grabbing him and dragging him down. I can only imagine the horror. The photos show a corpse with about a third to a half of the body missing and a face barely recognizable, twisted by agony with much of the flesh torn away. Noey said he would lie awake thinking about all the what-ifs. What could Kenton have done differently? Noey had found a pocket knife on Kenton. Why didn't he use it? Why did he run? Kenton's tracks ended where he had apparently stood on the shore of the lake, and there were wolf tracks coming toward that point. There was a clear line of sight from there to the Points North camp. Was Kenton yelling for help and no one heard him over the distance and the wind?

Mingled with images of Kenton's remains were images of the wolves Noey had chased with a snow machine and the one that had turned back on him. It scared him to think how differently that might have turned out.

Noey would get up in the middle of the night and pour him-self a large shot of whiskey, something to slow the thoughts, to let him sleep in peace.

Increased anxiety and depression are some of the symptoms of trauma. Alcohol relieves the anxiety. The problem with it, however, is that, because tolerance increases with use, more and more alcohol is required for the same relief. Noey's reliance on alcohol to medicate his symptoms of trauma eventually got out of hand. It almost cost him his career and his family.

He has been steadfastly sober now for several years.

SUSPECTS: TWO WOLVES ARE TAKEN

Two days after Kenton was found, SERM conservation officers Kelly Crane and Mario Gaudet—stationed in Southend, about two hundred kilometres south—arrived at Points North. They interviewed Mark Eikel and obtained background informa-tion about Kenton and the November 8 incident. Both officers then went to the scene, reporting, "Officers investigated the site and found numerous wolf tracks in the area. No other large animal tracks could be found."

Crane and Gaudet issued a nuisance wildlife permit to Eikel, Burseth, Ed Castle, and Andy Eikel. The control permit, issued November 10, 2005, authorized these men to "con-trol the following wildlife species: WOLF, by the following methods: SHOOTING for the purpose of eliminating property damage by these animals." The permit stated the follow-ing conditions: "All wildlife regulations apply. All persons on the permit must have a valid firearms licence. Southend Conservation Officers must be notified if a wolf has been shot.

Permit is only valid within the immediate area." Signed by
conservation officer Gaudet, the permit had an expiry date of
March 31, 2006.

On November 11, Burseth shot two wolves. On November
15, those wolves were picked up by the Southend conservation officers. On November 16, the wolves were transported
to the Western College of Veterinary Medicine in Saskatoon.
On November 18, necropsies were conducted on the two
wolves shot by Burseth. For both wolves, the procedure was
"observed by Dr. Ernie Walker, Department of Anthropology,
U of S and also of the RCMP, and by Dr. Paul Paquet, wolf
specialist, University of Calgary."

Both wolves were adult males, one estimated to be four
to five years old and the other over five years old. The necropsy reports for both wolves note that death resulted from a
gunshot and that no evidence of disease was found; in fact,
both wolves are described as being "in excellent nutritional
condition as evidenced by abundant body fat and full-sized
muscles." Both reports note that "Dr. Paquet also saw no evidence that the animal was a wolf-dog hybrid."

In both cases, no food or other material was found in the
animals' stomachs or small intestines, but the colon and rectum contained undigested material, including small hairs:
"Specimens have been retained that would permit assessment of the identity of the hairs found in the lower digestive
tract and also that would permit analysis of skin around muz-
zle and front feet for human DNA. Other tissues have been
retained for potential genetic analysis of the wolf."

The two necropsy reports contain the following statement:
"The Canadian Food Inspection Agency reports that the brain
of this wolf was examined for the presence of rabies virus and
that no rabies virus was detected."

Both reports are dated November 21, 2005, and are signed by veterinary pathologist Dr. Ted Leighton.

The short black twisted hairs found in the two wolves could have been from Kenton. If this could be proven, it would prove that the two wolves shot at Points North were the wolves responsible for his death. Both necropsy reports state that "no forensic testing will be undertaken until authorization and directions are received from appropriate authorities." The problem was who was going to pay for the additional testing. SERM thought the RCMP, or maybe the coroner's office, should pay for the testing. It took some time to sort things out, and the samples of hair were finally sent to the Molecular Diagnostic Division of Genetrack Biolabs, in Vancouver. It is unclear which department paid for the analysis.

The results of the DNA forensic identity test—dated March 13, 2006, reviewed by Dr. Edmond T. Wong, and sent to R. Kent Stewart, chief coroner—were that "the sample did not contain sufficient intact human DNA to yield a DNA profile."

Samples were then sent to the University of Victoria's Department of Biology. On June 8, 2006, Chris Darimont, then a PhD student in the department, wrote to Dr. Walker, one of the observers of the wolf necropsies:

> I have examined the hair samples you sent last week with a dissecting microscope and voucher hair specimens from most mammals in North America, including humans.
>
> I have concluded that the closest match is human hair, based on the following:
>
> 1. The hairs were generally consistent in coloration along the shaft.

2. Medulla length was less than one-third of the hair diameter.
3. Hairs were wavy. I know of no other North American mammals with curly or wavy hair. More over, I suspect that digestion could not have produced that effect, given the molecular-protein basis for curly hair. Also, over 4,000 hair samples my team and I have examined in wolf faeces, none have been curly.

Again, my conclusion is one of probability. To be certain, I recommend DNA analyses.

THE POST-INCIDENT REPORT

Because there has never been any official documentation of a human killed by wild wolves in North America, the coroner hired a wolf expert to investigate. The expert chosen was Paul Paquet from the University of Calgary, who had also observed the wolf necropsies.

The short version of Paquet's curriculum vitae runs twelve pages, with an impressive list of publications. His education includes degrees in philosophy, zoology, and biology. His graduate research examined aspects of social behaviour in captive wolves and, specifically in Riding Mountain National Park, Manitoba, behavioural ecology of sympatric (coexisting) wolves and coyotes. He has had academic appointments in biology, zoology, and environment and geography departments at the Universities of Alberta, Calgary, New Brunswick, and Manitoba, among others.

Paquet had access to all of the available information on the death of Kenton Carnegie, and he was present at the necropsies of the two wolves conducted ten days after Kenton's death.

A report co-authored by Paquet and Ernest G. Walker, forensic anthropologist at the University of Saskatchewan, was released on August 8, 2006. Walker has participated in many police investigations and is a special constable with the RCMP. He is highly respected by the legal community in Saskatchewan. Lawyers know that if they are relying on a report authored by Walker, the judge hearing their submissions is likely to be paying close attention, and opposing counsel is not likely to make arguments.

The Paquet-Walker report concluded that "the preponderance of indirect evidence suggests Carnegie was attacked and killed by a black bear rather than by wolves." This conclusion was based on six factors: bear tracks at the scene; the position of the body when found; the victim's clothes having been removed from the body; the dragging of the body; the feeding pattern; and the types of injuries. Indeed, the report noted, "All outside experts who examined the evidence concluded independently that the most probable predator was a black bear."

WHAT ABOUT THE BEAR TRACKS?

A single photo taken after Kenton Carnegie's death is the only evidence of bear tracks at the scene. And we have to be careful how we define the evidence found at the scene. These alleged bear tracks were photographed on the lake. Kenton's body was found inland. No indications of bear tracks are noted adjacent to where the body was first discovered or where it was finally recovered. This photograph was taken within a few hundred metres of those places but not directly adjacent to them.

Taken by Constable Noey the morning after the discovery of Kenton's body, the photo is from the south shore of the unnamed lake looking westward (Figure 7). It shows multiple animal tracks on the ice. The tracks in question are those that appear beginning near the bottom right corner and travelling toward the left across the bottom half of the photo. The tracks are quite pronounced.

The only person who has positively identified these tracks as bear tracks is Manitoba wildlife biologist Dr. Vince Crichton.

Lori Carnegie, the mother of Kenton, emailed Crichton on September 4, 2006. Her first email is quite general: "I believe you may have been consulted as an expert during the investigation of this incident. I am curious as to what information

Figure 7. Tracks in the snow near the death site, identified by Dr. Vince Crichton as bear tracks. (Photograph courtesy of Coroner's Office, Government of Saskatchewan.)

may have been shared with you and what contribution you made to this case."

Dr. Crichton replied as follows:

As the report has not hyet [sic; yet] been officially released I cannot report on the findings in it. I was coanted [sic; contacted] as aprofesional [sic; a professional] wildlife biologist and shown scenes of the attack. I was asked for my independent assessment based on what the photos showed at the scene of this most teagic [sic; tragic] event.

First of all, I noted there were tracks of different species of animals in some of the photos I was shown. I believe some were fox and in one photo the tracks were what I contend were bear tracks. Although there were certaily [sic; certainly] wolves present at the site I do not recll [sic; recall] seeing any tracks that I could say definitely were wolves. Further, I must tell you that I have not consulted my previous email based on my finding before replying to you.

I also noted with interest marks I saw on the body—the scratches seemed more in line with that which might be made by a bear and not wolves. I also noted that the body had been dragged as clothing was caught in a tree. This again suggests to me something that a bear might do and not wolves although, yes, on small items they might pull them away.

Based on my examination only of the photos death likely resulted from a black bear attack but one cannot definitely rule out wolves.

In closing I can appreciate the anxiety that you and your family are experiencing over this tragic event and you have my deepest sympathy.

Another exchange of emails occurred, with Lori asking a few more specific questions and Crichton replying. Then, quite late on September 6, 2006—the time stamp indicates 11:24 p.m.—Lori sent the following detailed list of questions:

How many bear prints did you observe in the photo?
    Were the bear print(s) clearly identifiable?
    Did the bear print(s) suggest the animal was walking, running or bounding?
    Were the prints made by the front or back paws of the bear?
    Were you provided with the necessary information to understand where this specific photo was taken?
    Where do you believe this bear print was in relation to the accident scene?
    Was it ever indicated to you that a bear may have been responsible for this attack before you were given an opportunity to make your own observations from the photos?
    Would you consider animal track identification an area of your expertise?
    Would you have come to the same conclusion about it being a bear attack if the bear prints were not found at the scene?
    Who provided you with the photos?
    On what part of Kenton's body were the scratches located as seen in the photos?
    Could the scratches on Kenton's body have been made by teeth rather than claws?

The following morning at 7:43 a.m., Crichton forwarded the above email to Paquet, one of the authors of the report, along with the following note: "Paul—need some advice—I am

leaning toward saying that because fo [sic; of] potential further
legal issues I cannot say anymore—also, are you in today—I
want to tlak [sic; talk] with you on another issue Vince."

It can be inferred from Paquet's curriculum vitae that he
and Crichton have a close relationship. In the list of publications, Crichton is listed as a co-author in one 1988 study of
cadmium levels in Manitoba wildlife. Most telling, however,
is that on the last page of Paquet's cv he lists Crichton as a
personal reference.

The biggest problem with the bear tracks is that no one
other than Crichton identified any tracks as belonging to a
bear. The first people on the scene were Eikel, Svarckopf, and
Van Galder. They reported seeing wolf tracks. None of these
men would describe themselves as experts on bear or wolf
tracks; they reported what they thought they saw. Burseth
was next on the scene. He has many years of experience in
the North and, even though he would not rate himself as an
expert, told me that he can tell the difference between a wolf
and a bear track. Burseth saw only wolf tracks. He did not see
any bear tracks.

Constable Noey arrived along with coroner Rosalie Tsannie-
Burseth. Neither of them saw bear tracks. Tsannie-Burseth is
from the Dene community of Wollaston Lake. She grew up in
this territory and told me that she does know the difference
between wolf and bear tracks. She observed the area. She
appears in several of Noey's photos, including one in which
she is seen looking closely at animal tracks (Figure 8).

Noey is from the far northern Dene community of Fond du
Lac. He grew up in the North. Noey photographed the area,
paying very close attention to the tracks as he investigated. He
didn't see any tracks that he identified as bear. In an interview,
Noey and I discussed what it means to be an expert tracker—we

Figure 8. Rosalie Tsannie-Burseth looking at animal tracks near the death scene. (Photograph courtesy of Coroner's Office, Government of Saskatchewan.)

both have the same definition, which excludes us. To us, an expert is someone, like Noey's father, who can not only tell the difference between a wolf and a bear track but also tell you how old the tracks are to the hour, how fast the animal was moving, its size, and the general state of the animal's health. While both Noey and I can distinguish between a wolf and a bear track, neither of us would claim to be an expert.

A couple of days after Noey investigated, the two conservation officers from SERM, Crane and Gaudet, searched the area. They saw only wolf tracks. As quoted earlier, they specifically stated, "Officers investigated the site and found numerous wolf tracks in the area. No other large animal tracks could be found." Presumably, conservation officers know the difference between wolf and bear tracks.

The snow conditions on November 8, 2005, were ideal for tracking. In fresh snow only a few centimetres deep, tracks are clear and precise. In deeper snow, the snow falls down into the track and blurs it.

Interestingly, in his email to Lori Carnegie, Crichton stated, "I do not recall seeing any tracks that I could say definitely were wolves." That is, he could not identify any of the multitude of clear tracks as those of wolves, but he could identify slushy tracks as caused by a bear.

Crichton is the only person involved in the investigation who cannot see wolf tracks. Based on Crichton alone, the Paquet-Walker report states that "the photographs of the site provided by Constable Noey also show the tracks of a bounding black bear together with tracks of walking wolves."

One photograph—photograph 70, the one relied upon by Crichton as showing bear tracks—has a clear impression of an obvious wolf track in the lower left corner. It should be safe to assume that Crichton paid very close attention to this photograph and examined it thoroughly to make his expert assessment.

PART 3

THE INQUEST

IT BEGINS

A coroner's inquest was opened into the death of Kenton Carnegie in Prince Albert, Saskatchewan, on November 1, 2007.

Dr. Vince Crichton of Manitoba Conservation was on the telephone to testify as an expert on bear tracks.

I represented the Carnegie family and cross-examined Crichton.

When I asked him about his expertise, he indicated that he was an expert on moose. I asked him how a moose expert could be an expert on bear tracks, and he replied that he had seen many bear tracks around moose kill sites.

I responded that I was a trapper and had seen lots of tracks in my life, but—

Then the attorney for the coroner stood up and objected, saying that it was improper for counsel to give evidence. All I'd intended to say in conclusion was that even though I had seen a lot of tracks I wouldn't call myself an expert.

Expertise is more than familiarity. To become an expert in law, or even in popular understanding, should require at least some dedicated study of the subject matter. Crichton hadn't done that. What appears to have happened is that one of the writers of the report, Paul Paquet, had called upon a friend, and the friend had given the opinion that was requested.

During cross-examination at the coroner's inquest, I asked Crichton whether he was able to discern the direction of travel of the alleged bear from the tracks. He wasn't able to. This inability to tell the direction of travel severely discredits him as an expert. Even when a track is so blurred that the toe marks are impossible to see, the drag marks tell the direction the animal was moving. The drag marks are always before the imprint. This isn't knowledge exclusive to experts. Most hunters know this. Yet Crichton hadn't looked closely enough at the photograph of the tracks to see the very apparent drag marks.

Mark E. McNay, a wildlife biologist for the Alaska Department of Fish and Game, Fairbanks, disagreed with Crichton as to the source of the tracks photographed on the lake. In a report prepared for the coroner's inquest, McNay used photographs to identify differences between the tracks of wolves and bears. The tracks of a running wolf are in sets of four, an almost straight-line grouping, with gaps of one to three metres between each set. A trotting wolf will leave a pattern of paired tracks with a gap of about two-thirds of a metre between each pair. A walking wolf will leave an almost straight-line pattern of tracks. In contrast, bear tracks exhibit a wider stance (Figure 9).

The tracks that Crichton identified as bear in the photograph have drag marks that indicate direction of travel (see Figure 7). The drag marks appear before each track and indicate an animal walking away from the shore toward the open lake. As the animal leaves the shore and steps onto the lake, it steps into snow with a layer of water between the surface of the snow and the underlying ice. The tracks have no particular pattern at first but quickly become typical of a trotting wolf, as though the animal suddenly found itself with its feet in cold water and trotted away to get out of the slush.

Following the tracks from the shore, the animal walks out onto the lake, finds its feet in cold water, turns toward its left, and trots parallel to the shore. Following the tracks farther out onto the lake, once the trotting animal reaches drier snow it turns toward its right, leaving tracks typical of a wolf. At this point, once the animal is out of the slush, the tracks become smaller. It is because the pronounced tracks in the photograph were made in slush and are filled with water that they appear larger. At the bottom right corner of the photograph, there is a distinct wolf track in the snow covering a rock. This track is heading toward the lake. The only tracks on the lake that correspond with this track are the pronounced tracks.

The tracks that Crichton attributed to a bear begin as wolf tracks, transform into what he identified as bear, and then transform back into wolf tracks.

Figure 9. Walking wolf tracks (left) and walking bear tracks (right). (Source: University of Wisconsin Board of Regents on behalf of wuwm Radio [left] and Wikimedia Commons/Yellowstone National Park. Public domain [right].)

To be fair, distinguishing between wolf and bear tracks really doesn't require much expertise. The tracks are very different from each other. The most pronounced difference is that wolf tracks show four toes and bear tracks show five toes. On a bear, the front feet are distinct from the hind feet. Stephen Herrero, an actual expert on bears, explains, "Both black and grizzly bears have short, broad feet with five toes on both front and back feet. The front-paw track of a bear is different from the hind-paw track. Bears walk more on their front toes than on their front heel. The hind foot, however, typically shows both toe and heel imprints."

Bear tracks are usually larger than wolf tracks. Even the black bear common in northern Saskatchewan, which typically has a smaller imprint than the larger grizzly bear, leaves a track that is bigger than that of the average wolf. Wolves can leave impressive prints, though. I photographed a wolf track on November 6, 2016 (Figure 10). For scale, I placed a Leatherman multi-tool beside it that is about ten centimetres long. I took the photograph because I was impressed by the size and depth of the track. The ground was moist but not wet, yet the track was quite deep, indicating to me that the wolf must have been of a respectable weight.

A large adult male wolf might leave a track larger than a young bear, so we cannot say that bear tracks are always larger than wolf tracks. But the death of Kenton Carnegie occurred in November, when even a young bear would be quite large and no longer a cub.

Another significant difference between the tracks of a wolf and a bear is that the two centre toes of a wolf, or any canine, extend farther than the two outside toes. Bear tracks don't look like that. The toes of a bear on both the front and the rear feet form more of a straight line (Figure 11).

Figure 10. Wolf track with a Leatherman multi-tool beside it. The photograph was taken on provincial highway 969, a well-travelled road. Note the depth of track left by a passing automobile. (Photograph by author.)

Figure 11. Wolf tracks (left) and black bear tracks (right) in snow. (Photographs courtesy of Oregon Department of Fish and Wildlife [left] and Lynn Rogers/North American Bear Center [right].)

A bear's claws are used for climbing, and they extend out farther than those of a wolf. On a bear track, the claw marks will be farther from the toe imprint than on a wolf, which has shorter claws.

For a walking wolf, the rear foot steps into the track vacated by the front foot on the same side. Bears don't do that; their front and rear paw prints never overlap.

Given the significant differences between wolf and bear tracks, it is hard to imagine that of all the people who looked at the tracks—who studied the tracks trying to decipher what had happened—none of them saw a track significantly different from the predominant tracks made by wolves. If bear tracks had been mingled in with the wolf tracks, they would have been very apparent to anyone, whether they classified themselves as experts or not.

Paquet and Walker's report states, "Although quite prominent in the photographs, bear tracks were not mentioned in the RCMP report detailing examination of the accident scene. We believe this was an oversight owing to inexperience in identifying tracks of wild animals." Further, the authors point out that "photographs taken at the scene the same day by Noey show tracks of black bear and smaller mammals, likely foxes. Although the age of the tracks in the photographs cannot be determined, the failure to report their presence suggests a predetermined focus on wolves, an oversight in reporting, or inexperience in identifying tracks."

I contend there were no bear tracks at the scene. If there had been bear tracks anywhere in the area examined by multiple people looking specifically for tracks, someone would have noticed a track that was significantly different. True, there are fox tracks in the photos, and no one mentioned them. But a fox is a canine; its track is identical in shape and pattern as a wolf's, although smaller. People searching the area would have seen a significant amount of wolf tracks and some tracks that looked like wolf tracks but were smaller.

Paquet and Walker were critical of the expertise of the people who looked at the actual tracks in the snow and relied instead upon a moose expert who identified a bear track based on one photograph. Throughout their report the authors state that bear tracks were found at the scene as though that fact was well established and beyond any doubt. Those alleged bear tracks identified by Crichton form the cornerstone of the report's conclusion that Kenton Joel Carnegie "was attacked and killed by a black bear rather than by wolves."

THE CONDITION AND POSITION OF THE BODY

Despite citing the condition and position of the body when found as a factor in their determination of the cause of death, Paquet and Walker state with regard to this factor only that "the position and condition of the body when recovered matched other fatal attacks by bears and differed from what might be expected if wolves were responsible. The victim's limbs were not pulled away from the body as would likely occur if wolves had fed exclusively on the body." The authors cite a personal conversation with a D. Bibikov in support of this assertion. However, the appendices to the report do not list D. Bibikov in either Appendix 1, the list of experts consulted, or the list "Literature, Statements and Reports" starting on page 24.

My own research indicates that Dimitri Ivanovic Bibikov was born in 1916 and died in 1997. His work *Der Wolf (Canis lupus)* was published in 1988. Therefore, unless the authors of the report had a time machine, they did not have a personal conversation with Bibikov about the position and location of Kenton Carnegie's body.

The photographs of Kenton's body taken by Constable Noey clearly show him flat on his back in the snow, both of his legs extended parallel to each other with the pant leg caught on a stump, with his right arm at an angle primarily over his head. His left arm, while covered by clothing and not visible, is obviously outstretched under the clothing because it does not appear in the space between the clothing and the side of the body. The assertion by Paquet and Walker that "the victim's limbs were not pulled away from the body" is simply not true. Noey took fifteen photographs of Kenton's body at the scene, and the authors of the report had access to all of them. Of none of them can it be said that his limbs were not pulled away from the body.

The photographs that Noey took of Kenton's body where he found him are difficult to look at. They show a young man on his back in the snow with large sections of his body eaten away, exposing the underlying flesh. His eyes are open, and most of his right cheek and throat is missing. The ribs on the right side are exposed and bare. Most of the abdomen is gone, and internal organs are visible.

I now tell young lawyers, "Don't look at the pictures if you don't have to."

After twenty years of practice and reviewing too many autopsy and crime scene photographs, my tolerance for the gruesome has been diminished. A sensitivity seems to have built up over the years. I can't say that any one photo booklet was harder to view than any other. It was all of them. But the eighty-one photographs taken at the scene and the fifty-seven photographs of the autopsy of Kenton Carnegie were among the hardest to look at.

If I were a little more callous, I might have included them in this book, sensationalized the story, used the human factor (many people like to see horror and are drawn to it) to draw attention to the work.

Most of the reason I am not including those photographs, which are not necessary to tell the story, is out of respect for Kenton. He should not be remembered in that position. He should be remembered as a young man furthering his education and looking toward a life of promise.

When a photograph is necessary, it has been edited to show only what is necessary.

WHAT HAPPENED TO KENTON'S CLOTHING?

The report prepared by Paquet and Walker for the coroner states that "most of Carnegie's clothes were removed from his body and inverted in a manner similar to the stripping of hides frequently observed when bears kill and consume ungulates." It goes on as follows:

> Stripping of clothes from the body is consistent with documented bear attacks elsewhere (S. Hererro pers. comm., W. McCrory pers. comm., M. de Almeida pers. comm.). Black bears often fully invert the hide of their prey and pull it off the carcass. From our records of kills made by black bears, full inversion of the hide occurred in about 105 (88%) of 199 documented cases (n=119). By comparison, wolves fully inverted the hide of 1 white-tailed deer (*O. virginianus*) and partially inverted the hides of 15

other deer and elk (n=1,496). We have no recorded wolf kills where hides of ungulates have been totally peeled off and fully inverted. In addition, researchers elsewhere have not observed this behaviour by wolves (L. Mech pers. comm., M. Jimenez pers. comm., D. Smith pers. comm., A. Wydevent pers. comm.). Our best understanding of wolves feeding on clothed human bodies is that they rip and tear the clothes away (D. Bibikov pers. comm., Y. Jhala pers. comm.).

Mark McNay, the wildlife biologist from Alaska, wrote a report at the behest of the Carnegie family. His interpretation of the photographs differs starkly from Paquet and Walker's:

Most of the victim's clothes remained with the body but torn pieces of clothing were scattered nearby as seen in Photos 957 and 959. Mr. Carnegie was wearing lined "sweat pants" and did not wear a belt. It is evident that Mr. Carnegie's pants (photo 922) were snagged on a tree stump of approximately 10–15 cm diameter while the body was being dragged. As a result, the pants were pulled tight around the ankles. The inversion of the pants undoubtedly resulted from the body being dragged over the tree stump. In Photo 922 [Figure 12] it is apparent that considerable tension in the stretched pant leg remained when the body was found, suggesting the body had been pulled to a stop just prior to its discovery. Significant movement and feeding on the body would have likely caused a relaxation of the tension in the pant leg.

The peeling of clothing referred to by Paquet and Walker (2006:19) occurred when the pants were snagged on a small tree stump while the body was being dragged.

Considerable tension remained on the pant leg when the body was found, indicating little movement of the body occurred after the pants were pulled tight.

Although in some cases bears have stripped clothing from victims, in other cases they have not (Hererro 1985). For example, in a June 2006 incident where a grizzly bear killed and fed upon a man and woman in northern Alaska, the man's body was largely stripped of clothing, but the woman's body was not. Over a 2-day period, the bear fed on the woman's hips, buttocks and ribs, but the woman's pants and shirt remained in place on her body. (Appendix E: Figure 30). We know little about patterns of clothing removal in cases where wolves killed and fed upon humans. Where wolves scavenged soldiers killed in battle, Paquet and Walker (2006) cite an undocumented reference to Bibikov (1983) which presumably describes clothing being torn from bodies, but the pattern of

Figure 12. Kenton Carnegie's pant leg caught on a tree stump. (Photograph courtesy of Coroner's Office, Government of Saskatchewan.)

removing a belted, heavy woolen uniform from a corpse that was exposed to unknown levels of damage, decomposition or rigor mortis, may not be indicative of what would occur if wolves fed on a recently killed human who was wearing loose fitting clothes made of lightweight, synthetic fabric. In the case of Kenton Carnegie, it is apparent that the pants were pulled to the ankles as a result of being dragged. Clothing from the upper part of the body was pulled up around the neck and left shoulder, some of the clothing had been ripped and torn from the body (Photos 957 and 959). Mr. Carnegie wore no belt and multiple layers of loose clothing, the clothing would easily have been pulled off with minimal tearing by either wolves or a bear.

As shown in the excerpt above, Paquet and Walker cited a personal communication with M. de Almeida as their source for the assertion that "stripping of clothes from the body is consistent with documented bear attacks elsewhere." Their report lists Maria de Almeida, large carnivores biologist, of the Ontario Ministry of Natural Resources in Appendix 1 as one of the experts consulted.

In response to an inquiry from Brent R. Patterson, a research scientist with the Ontario Ministry of Natural Resources, de Almeida explained the following in an email:

Paul [Paquet] has clarified that I was mentioned in the Coroner's report because there was a commitment to reference in the coroner's report any discussion that investigators had on the case with individuals as personal communication. Somehow "personal communication" became "consultant" in the final report. I was included because when I spoke to Paul about public education in the spring, he mentioned to me that there was evidence of the victim's clothes having been rolled back and I discussed with him some of the bear fatalities in Ontario. I was not asked to review any evidence related to the case.

Interestingly, Dr. Patterson is not included in the list of experts consulted in the Paquet-Walker report even though he was consulted. Patterson wrote a brief report at the behest of the Carnegie family, which included the following paragraph:

During our phone conversation of 10 October 2006 I was told by Paul Paquet that the predator that killed Kenton was strong enough to break his belt when the belt snagged on a stump while his body was being dragged. This conversation occurred before I had examined most of the evidence cited above and I did not question his statement. The broken belt was taken as evidence that a bear, rather than wolves, was responsible for dragging Kenton's body post-mortem. However, I observed no evidence of a belt in any of the RCMP photos, and as far as I can tell from photos Kenton was wearing lined Nylon pants which generally do not even have belt loops. Further, there was no mention of a belt in the listing of Kenton's personal effects at the time of the necropsy by Cst. Steven (contained in document #4 cited above). Thus it seems unlikely that Kenton was even wearing a belt when he was killed.

The omission of Patterson from the list of experts consulted by Paquet and Walker leaves room to wonder whether only those experts who agreed with the authors were included.

With regard to the removal of clothing during feeding, Patterson wrote,

> Paquet and Walker (2006) state that much of Kenton's clothing was removed consistent with what would be expected had a bear been feeding on his body (i.e. "removed and inverted in a manner similar to the stripping of hides"), but inconsistent with what would be expected from wolves. Although I cannot rule out the possibility that Kenton's pants were peeled off first and then later snagged on the stump during dragging, it is clear from the photographs that the "removal" of his pants could have occurred entirely as a result of snagging on the small stump (clearly indicated in photo 922) as his body was being drug. I saw no other evidence of clothing having been "peeled" off rather than simply ripped or torn during feeding.

Despite the Paquet-Walker report's assertion that the clothing was peeled rather than torn from Kenton's body, the photographs taken by Constable Noey suggest something different. Noey documented tracks made by both Kenton and the pursuing wolves. He inferred from a disturbed patch of snow with multiple tracks that the wolves had first made contact with Kenton in that location. He then followed the tracks to the location where the body was first observed by Eikel and later confirmed by Eikel and Burseth. Noey took five photographs of this scene. In three of those photos a torn piece of clothing is shown adjacent to the blood-saturated snow where the body obviously had lain and was fed upon. Another piece of clothing appears in a photograph Noey took of the drag marks somewhere between the first and second body locations. Clearly, in the first instance the wolves had torn the clothing from the body.

A QUESTION OF DRAGGING

The Paquet-Walker report relies on the fact that Kenton's body was dragged to conclude that the animal responsible was a bear. The report states,

> In addition, the body was dragged from where Carnegie died 50–60m up a slight hill and through muskeg, deadfalls, small trees, and shrubs. With natural prey, dragging of large bodies is a characteristic behaviour of bears but not wolves. Wolves commonly carry small prey (5–10kg) such as deer fawns (*Odocoileus sp.*) and caribou (*Rangifer tarandus*) calves away from the site of attack before killing them. (Pers. observation) Likewise, in India small children preyed upon by wolves are often carried away from the attack site (Rajurohit 1999, Jhala pers. comm). Two or more wolves are certainly capable of dragging a 70kg body more than 50m. In our experience, however, when more than 1 wolf is involved in a kill of a large bodied animal (>40kg), dragging is seldom directionally coordinated because individual wolves usually tug from different directions. From our records of more than 1,500 deer, elk (*Cervus elaphus*), moose and caribou killed by wolves, dragging the carcass more than 10m occurred less than 1% of the time. The longest straight-line drag distance recorded was about 32m, and this was a deer carcass placed on a frozen lake as bait. In comparison, nearly all of the 119 bear kills of elk and moose we investigated

showed signs of dragging, although distances were more difficult to determine because of the absence of snow. Nevertheless, bears moved many carcasses more than 50m. U.S. Fish and Wildlife records of large carnivores dragging carcasses support our observations. Of 300 recorded kills, in only 4 cases did wolves drag ungulate carcasses in the snow more than 10m. All the bear kills located were dragged some distance (>30m) away from where the initial fatal attack occurred (M. Jimenez and E. Bangs pers. comm.). Based on examination of 2,173 wolf kills in Yellowstone National Park, Wyoming, dragging of carcasses was an extremely rare phenomenon and never exceeded 15m (D. Smith pers. comm.).

At this point in reviewing the Paquet-Walker report, I am struck by the extreme number of personal communication citations. They are troublesome because they are extremely difficult to verify. I would have to contact each of the persons cited and ask specifically what they might have told the report writers. The use of personal communication citations becomes even more problematic when one of the persons cited turns out to have died several years before the report was written (Bibikov), another only spoke to one of the authors for a few minutes and was never shown the evidence (de Almeida), and an expert who was in personal communication with one of the authors but disagreed with the assessment was not cited (Patterson). Also, one of the report's authors gave Patterson false information about Kenton wearing a belt in an obvious attempt to influence his opinion in favour of a bear as the attacker.

With regard to dragging the body, the report writers chose to use the maximum distance reported. The estimate of fifty to sixty metres comes from the statement given by Robert Burseth to Constable Noey at 3:07 p.m. on November 9, the day after the incident:

> NOEY: And from the time you went in the first time yourself till when you came back with us ahm...was everything still the same?

> BURSETH: [unintelligible] you guys were there, 60, 50–60 yards maybe.

Earlier in the same interview, Burseth made another estimate of distance, from where they had parked the truck to where they first saw the body. This time, however, he qualified the estimate based upon it being dark.

> BURSETH: Oh, the distance we walked from the truck?

> NOEY: Yeah.

> BURSETH: Oh, that would be, 100, 150 yards? Something like that. It seems a lot longer at night than [unintelligible].

Page 9 of the Paquet-Walker report states, "The body was dragged another 50–60m straight-line distance to where Constable Noey first saw the body." Nowhere does Burseth say that the fifty to sixty metres was a straight-line distance. This estimate was made during the course of an interview after a traumatic day. It was also made at the Points North camp, away from the scene. In giving the estimate, Burseth must have relied upon memories laid down either at night when distances are very hard to judge or when he went out the next day with Noey and Tsannie-Burseth and stood guard with a rifle as they examined the scene.

Noey gave two divergent estimates of the distance the body was dragged. In his report he estimated the distance to be fifty metres:

> Member noted foot prints on shore line walking south bound with wolf tracks heading in the same direction (wolf tracks over the foot tracks). Looked like the wolf followed or stalked CARNEGIE from time he left the PNC site. Member followed tracks past body site location. Footprints went for another 60–80 meters south where he stood near shoreline where he may have been trying to get someone's attention from PNC as you have a clear line of sight to PNC. At that location member noted more wolf tracks coming towards foot tracks where he may have been standing. Wolf tracks were coming from lake and south toward where he was standing. At this point foot prints turned back toward road. About 10–20 meter[s] north along the trail snow on ground was disturbed indicating some sort of altercation. Foot trail showed him going through the trail and partly into the muskeg. Member followed more foot tracks going north to where blood was found along with pieces of clothing. Near a small tree member saw what looked like someone standing and blood dripping on ground. Near that site is where more blood was found. This is possible the kill site and where the body was 1st seen by searchers. Body was dragged another 50 meter[s] through the muskeg to where member 1st seen the body. Member took pictures of scene until battery in camera died. Member searched area for more evidence but none found. All clothing seized by member. Pieces of pants and jacket consistent with what member found on body.

However, the map Noey prepared shows the distance at just twenty metres. This is the distance between point 5 and point 6.

I asked Noey about distances during my interview with him on February 3, 2018. I did not have his report or his map to put in front of him, and he did not have an answer for the discrepancy. We were sitting in a Boston Pizza in Melfort. Noey took a bit of time, trying to remember, and then said, "The entire area I investigated wasn't any bigger than this room." I looked around. It was a large restaurant. I reimagined it snow-covered with small pine trees, shrubs, and muskeg. The room was definitely big enough to encompass the area indicated on Noey's map. I could imagine the area of disturbed snow where it looked like the wolves first brought Kenton down—tracks leading from there to the point where he was brought down the second time, where Eikel and Van Galder and Svarckopf first found him—drag marks to the final location, where Noey found and photographed him. It was a large restaurant, but not large enough to contain drag marks stretching fifty metres.

The problem with the Paquet-Walker assertion quoted above that "two or more wolves are certainly capable of dragging a 70kg body more than 50m" is that Kenton's body would no longer have weighed the estimated seventy kilograms. According to "Preliminary Anatomic Diagnosis: Consistent with an Animal Attack" by Dr. Nico Brits, the pathologist who conducted the autopsy on November 9, 2005,

> The body was that of a Young Man with a length Approximately 174 cm and he was Well Built and Fairly Muscular. It is difficult to Estimate His Weight Due to large Areas of Tissue Loss....The Soft Tissue From the Right Side of the Scalp and Lower Part of the Right Side of the Face, the Anterior

and Lateral Aspects of the Neck, the Anterior Chest Wall up to the Ribcage. The Left Half of the Chest Showed Intact Skin. There was Tissue Loss from the Right Upper Arm, the Whole of the Abdominal Wall and all Abdominal Organs Except for Part of the Liver, Prostate, Part of the Bladder and a small Piece of Rectum. There were Large Areas of Tissue Loss from the Pelvis and the Thighs up to the Knees, a Large Area of Tissue Loss was Present on the Lateral Aspect of the Left Lower Leg Involving the Middle Third of the Lower Leg. A bruise was found on the Right Shin Measuring 4X2.5 cm. On Turning the Body Over, there was Extensive Loss of Soft Tissue from the Mid Back, the Buttocks and the Thighs Up To the Back of the Knees and the Right Upper Arm. There was Skin and Soft Tissue Present on the Upper Back and Shoulders Showing Superficial Scrapes....The External Genitalia was Completely Lost Together with the Soft Tissue on the Pelvis. (All capitalization in original.)

Burseth described to Noey the condition of Kenton's body the first time he saw it as having been fed upon from the waist up. When asked specifically by Noey if the pants were still on, Burseth answered, "It looked like they were." Keep in mind that he only observed the body in this first instance from a distance in the dark with a flashlight. Burseth was also present at the final position, and he noted that much more feeding had occurred since he had first viewed the body. When asked by Noey about the condition of the body at its final location, Burseth answered, "Well, I believe there was more ah...'cause when we picked up the body, it was...there was no clothes right down to the...like to the knees, the flesh was gone and when I first seen it, it didn't look like as much."

Roughly a third to half of Kenton's body had been consumed. If he weighed seventy kilograms before the attack,
he certainly did not weigh that amount while he was being
dragged. Most of the feeding on Kenton's body would have
occurred at the original site rather than at the site where the
body was ultimately located.

McNay's report examined the evidence available from the
photographs of that final site:

> Much of the fresh snow on the small trees to the left of the
> body (i.e., left side of Photo 927) and beyond the head of
> the body was undisturbed (photo 923) indicating there
> had been minimal animal activity around the body after
> it was dragged. Branches of small ground shrubs were not
> trampled and the head of the victim was lying underneath
> small branches, dried leaves remained on the branches
> that extended over the body also indicating minimal dis-
> turbance and trampling around the body (Photos 942 and
> 935). Again this evidence indicates the body was dragged
> to its final position after it had been fed upon, and signifi-
> cant feeding on the victim had not occurred after the body
> was dragged.

McNay further noted, as evidence that the body had been
recently dragged to this last position, the fact that there was
still tension in the pant leg that was snagged on a stump. If
there had been feeding on the body, the actions would have
continuously shifted the body, and the pant leg would no longer have been taut.

In comparison, photos of the first site show small vegetation without snow cover near the bloodstained snow, and the
area appears much more trampled. This is the position where

torn clothing matching what Kenton was wearing was found and photographed by Noey.

Noey's description of position 5 on his map was as follows: "Run to this point. Half on the trail & half in the muskeg. Lots of disturbance in snow. Lots of blood. One area showed blood drops. May have stood there bleeding. Kill site. This is where 1st party saw body (Eikel)."

The snow conditions that evening would have been perfect for dragging. The weather was relatively warm. If it had been -30 or -40 degrees Celsius, as is possible at that time of year in northern Saskatchewan, the snow would have been much drier and not as lubricating as the warmer snow of November 8, 2005. As anyone who uses a kicksled, a dog team, or cross-country skis knows, cold snow is not as slippery as warmer snow.

The depth of the snow was also perfect: just enough to cover the ground and provide a slippery surface, without being too deep and thus an impediment to dragging. A few centimetres of relatively warm snow would have been of tremendous assistance in dragging Kenton's body twenty to fifty metres.

The Paquet-Walker report's assertion that "the body was dragged from where Carnegie died 50–60 m up a slight hill and through muskeg, deadfalls, small trees, and shrubs" is misleading. It suggests that the terrain would have been difficult. My assessment is that the photographs indicate otherwise. Not only is the distance of fifty to sixty metres in question, and the fact that snow conditions would have assisted not mentioned, but "the muskeg, deadfalls, small trees, and shrubs" are in actuality of a very low density. This part of northern Saskatchewan is primarily sand, covered by a few centimetres of topsoil. Trees and plants do not grow very well here. The most common ground cover is moss, which even without snow can be slippery. The muskeg is not like the deep bogs of farther south with large hummocks. It is relatively flat. The shrubs are dispersed and never grow thickly together. This is in no way dense undergrowth.

None of the deadfall indicated in the photographs appears much larger than fifteen centimetres in diameter because none of the trees in this area is any larger than that. All of the deadfall I saw in the photographs was very close to the ground and could be stepped over. The relative scarcity of trees meant there was little for deadfall to hang up on.

The slight hill mentioned in the report does not appear in any of the photographs. Constable Noey took seven photographs of what he called "drag marks." None of these photos indicates anything that could be considered a hill, not even a slight hill. The only land formation in that area that can be described as anything resembling a hill is the higher ground adjacent to the lake, and the body was not dragged in that direction. It was dragged parallel to the lake. The "slight hill" seems at best to be a misinterpretation of the evidence and at worst a complete fabrication.

After interviewing Noey I am more inclined to believe that the "slight hill" mentioned in the report is a complete fabrication. Noey said there was no hill, that the area was very flat, and if there was any change in elevation it wouldn't have been more than a foot.

Brent Patterson, while agreeing that "it may seem unusual for wolves, and typical for bears, to drag the carcass of a prey animal," wrote,

During our research into predator-prey interactions between wolves and their ungulate prey in Algonquin Park, and the Horwood Lake area, west of Timmins,

Ontario, wolves have been observed to kill and consume their prey in undisturbed areas, and subsequently to feed on the carcass at the immediate kill site. However, we have observed deer carcasses drug off of lakes into the woods in areas of high human use. Even in "remote" areas of Algonquin we have documented cases where wolves have drug deer carcasses 10–30 meters to a place more suitable for feeding. For example, a large white-tailed buck killed on the edge of a swale near Louisa Lake, Algonquin Park, in winter 2006 was drug into the centre of the opening prior to feeding. My students were tracking the wolves and examined the carcass within an hour or 2 of its having been killed.

McNay, who has done considerable research into wolf attacks on humans, wrote the following in his report prepared at the request of the Carnegie family:

Although wolves do not typically drag large prey away from a kill site, wolves are capable of dragging their prey and in cases where wolves seriously attacked humans, they attempted to drag or carry their "prey" as rescuers approached (McNay 2002a: Cases 1, 4, 15, 16, and 17). Similarly, in 195 cases of predation by wolves on children in India the children were carried as far as 2.5km from the attack site. Some of those victims were equal to half the wolf's body weight (Rajpurohit 1999). Clearly, in the case of the attacks and with small natural prey (Fox 1971), wolves often carry their prey away from the attack site.

Wolves are also capable of carrying or dragging prey of weights equal to or greater than their own. For example, in September 2006 near McGrath, Alaska, ADF&G [Alaska

Department of Fish and Game] research biologist Mark Keech walked in on the signal of a radio collared moose calf killed by 2 wolves. The calf remains, weighing approximately 150 lb, had recently been dragged 20 m up hill over dry ground from the kill site, possibly in response to the biologist's approach.

Based on my review of the photographs, my familiarity with the territory (having worked and lived in this part of the Athabasca Basin for more than a decade), my having dragged objects such as deer and logs through snow of varying depths at various temperatures, and my use of a kicksled, dog teams, and cross-country skis, I am quite certain that one of my sleigh dogs could have dragged that weight that distance in those conditions. My biggest sleigh dog would be only two-thirds the size of an average wolf.

What appears to have happened is that the wolves killed Kenton at the site marked as 5 on Noey's map. Here they fed extensively upon the body and in doing so trampled down the vegetation and tore away some of his clothing. Eikel, Van Galder, and Svarckopf disturbed the wolves at about 7:00 p.m. Eikel and Burseth returned a half-hour later and again disturbed the feeding. They viewed the body from a distance, noting that feeding had occurred from the waist upward. The wolves were then left in relative peace to feed until Noey, Tsannie-Burseth, Eikel, and Burseth returned again at about 9:50 p.m. The wolves had a little less than two and a half hours undisturbed at the original site. They would have had no reason to move their "prey" during that period. They were next disturbed when Noey and the rest of the party approached. It is quite possible that the wolves were dragging the body as the people approached.

More recent evidence shows that wolves do drag human prey. At approximately 5:00 p.m. on March 8, 2010, Candice Berner went jogging. An hour later her body was discovered next to a snow-covered road approximately three kilometres from the community of Chignik Lake, Alaska. The Alaska Department of Fish and Game (ADF&G) and Alaska State Troopers (AST) evaluated both the physical evidence and the eyewitness testimony of Chignik Lake residents. The investigators concluded that Berner had been attacked and killed by wolves. Genetic analysis of samples taken from the victim's clothing and from wolves that were killed near the scene positively identified one wolf and implicated others in the attack.

A detailed investigation showed that Berner's body was moved twice by the wolves. The first time it was dragged eighty-three feet (25.3 m), and the second time it was dragged a further seventy feet (21.3 m). As stated in the ADF&G report,

> The wolves initially moved her body downhill 83 feet from the location of her death...to the place where her body was first discovered...by the party of four returning from Dorner Bay. This movement occurred post-mortem as evidenced by a drag mark measuring two feet wide and one foot deep and without signs of a struggle. Earphones and a lycra-type garment were recovered by AST approximately 50 feet from the location of her death....There was very little snow melt at the site where her body was discovered, which suggests that her body had remained at the first site long enough to lose external body heat. The interviews and pictures taken the night of her death support the conclusion that wolves dragged the body downhill after she died (ADF&G interviews and AST report). The movement also explains why clothing was displaced when it was discovered, either by

the action of wolves pulling on it or by resistance caused by the snow. The body was moved a second time, after it had been discovered. Drag marks and a third depression in the snow...indicated that the body was moved north 70 feet downhill between the time it was initially discovered by the party of 4 returning from Dorner Bay (approximately 6:00 p.m.) and the time it was recovered and transported from the area by community residents. First-hand accounts from people present the night of the attack verified that her body was moved after its initial discovery (ADF&G interviews and AST report). Those witnesses also reported that a single wolf was observed at the location...that night.

THE FEEDING PATTERN

I have never seen a fresh wolf kill site. By the time I have ever found one, it was old, and it was difficult to determine exactly what had been killed and consumed. The only evidence was usually packed bloody snow and a few hair clumps, usually of moose. Therefore, I will leave this portion of the conversation about the feeding patterns of wolves entirely up to the experts.

With regard to the feeding pattern, the Paquet-Walker report states,

Wolf attacks on humans are rare in North America; fatal attacks by wild wolves are unknown. Because predation of humans by wolves is extremely uncommon, we have little information regarding details of predatory feeding behaviour. Almost all documented fatal attacks by non-rabid wolves are on children. Consequently, we cannot describe characteristic lethal injuries of fatal attacks.

From rabies cases, however, a very high percentage of attacks were directed at the head and face, which explains the high rates of mortality. In contrast, documented bite wounds that resulted from non-lethal attacks by wolves on humans vary considerably regarding the location of the injuries on the victim's bodies. We found no documentation of wounds resulting from clawing by wolves.

Bibikov (1983) provided details of wolves scavenging bodies of soldiers in Russia during World War II. On bodies that were not frozen, wolves ripped away clothes and with few exceptions fed "preferentially" on internal organs except the stomach and intestines. On bodies not recovered for burial, all of the large muscle masses were consumed and the bodies disarticulated and scattered about. He noted that foxes and avian scavengers also fed on the bodies.

With ungulate prey, wolves feed preferentially on the viscera and hind limbs. Except for stomach contents, carcasses might be entirely consumed. If the animal is attacked by a pack, the entire carcass is usually consumed quickly. This is especially true for young or small animals. The pattern is the same for wolves feeding on black bears, dogs and pinnipeds [seals]. Except for small prey, wolves usually consume their prey at the site where the animal was killed. It is extremely rare for wolves to drag remains more than a few meters from where an animal died. In contrast with bears, wolves that feed extensively typically disarticulate and scatter the remains of their prey. They do not cover bodies as with bears, vegetation (or snow) around the kill site is usually matted down by wolves. Feces, urine marks, and bed sites are usually found nearby.

In contrast, consider the following excerpt from McNay's report:

The skeletal structure of Kenton Carnegie's body was not damaged, there were no broken bones, skull punctures, or displaced vertebrae. There was no sign of penetrating or blunt injury into the chest cavity or into the cranial cavity. The autopsy report noted that there was skin and soft tissue remaining on the upper back and shoulders with multiple superficial scrapes, but those scrapes were not identified as claw marks (Appendix A: Document 17). Those superficial scrapes would be expected if the body was dragged across the ground. In a separate report, "furrows," one on the nose and one above the left eyebrow, were identified as being consistent with claw marks (Appendix A: Document 2). A portion of Mr. Carnegie's face had been removed and the small cuts on the intact portions of his face could have been [from] either claws or teeth, but furrows on the bridge of the nose and around the eyes as seen in Photo 935 are not consistent with deep slashing marks of bear claws inflicted during the predation phase of an attack (Appendix E: Figures 27 and 28). The furrows could be claw marks incidental to feeding, but are also consistent with small tooth inflicted lesions documented in other wolf attacks (Appendix D: Figure 25).

The remains of a completely consumed wolf kill is often scattered and the skeletal structure is at least partially disarticulated. However, wolves cannot disarticulate the skeleton of large prey until most of the muscle mass has been removed, therefore disarticulation would commonly occur 1 to several days after a kill, except on small prey. Both bears and wolves eat the internal organs....

[P]rey killed by wolves often has tissue removed from various parts of the body. For example, Magoun (1976) observed 2 wolves feeding on a fresh caribou carcass: in 2 hours meat from the back, the ribs, and the legs were eaten as well as portions of the internal organs. Depending on the size of the wolf pack and the size of the prey, large ungulates can be consumed by wolves in a few days or it may take a week or more....

With large ungulate prey, wolves do not eat the stomach contents because it consists of masticated vegetation which is inedible to wolves, but wolves do eat the stomach tissue (Peterson and Cuicci 2003: 123). In my experience in Alaska, when wolves consume other carnivores (e.g., wolves, lynx, wolverine), stomach contents are normally eaten. Paquet and Walker (2006: 16) cite an undocumented reference to Bibikov (1983) that described consumption by wolves of the bodies of soldiers killed in Russia during war. Allegedly, wolves in those cases did not feed on the stomach or intestines of the dead soldiers. Lack of feeding on the gut content in those cases may have been related to putrefaction; it is unknown when those soldiers were killed, how long before they were scavenged, and at what ambient temperatures. Therefore the implication that feeding on the stomach contents of a human is not a wolf trait is not well founded. In the Carnegie case, the body was freshly killed and the stomach contents would be entirely edible since Mr. Carnegie had presumably eaten earlier in the day, and the wolves were conditioned to eating human foods.

The feeding on Kenton Carnegie's body was extensive, most of the viscera (including the stomach) below the diaphragm was eaten, and a large portion of the muscle mass from the ribs to the knees was consumed. Mr. Carnegie's remains were not weighed at the autopsy, but from the photographs it appears that over half of the tissue body mass of the victim was removed. Mr. Carnegie's live weight was approximately 145 lb (Lori Carnegie, personal communication). Although it remains unknown, I estimate that roughly 70–80 lb of the body weight had been removed. It is unlikely that a single black bear would have removed that amount of tissue with the known time frame of 5 hours.

Studies of maximum consumption rates in brown bears indicate a bear could consume up to 15% of its body weight in a 24-hour period and that amount of food could be digested in as little as 12 hours by an extremely hungry bear (Dr. Charles Robbins, Professor, Washington State University, personal communication). Maximum consumption of approximately 7% of a bear's body weight would be expected during a 4–5 hour period (John Hectel, ADF&G biologist, personal communication). A large 300 lb bear therefore would eat about 21 lb in 4–5 hours, far less than was removed from Kenton Carnegie's body. Therefore, the amount of tissue loss and the patterns of tissue removal from multiple sites as shown in the RCMP Photos 934, 937, and 929 are most consistent with simultaneous feeding by multiple predators. Wolves can consume 15–20 lb each during a single feeding bout (Peterson and Ciucci 2003:124) so the amount of tissue loss from Mr. Carnegie's body in this case is consistent with feeding by 2–4 wolves.

With regard to the feeding pattern of wolves, Patterson stated in his short report,

I observed nothing in the photos of Kenton's body that could be used as evidence against wolves having fed on the body, or of bear(s) being more likely than wolves to have fed on his body. Paquet and Walker (2006: page 16) assert that the fact that Kenton's body was not disarticulated is evidence against wolves being the primary predator feeding on his body. Although wolves commonly disarticulate prey, this does not occur right away. Upon making a kill, wolves will generally feed until full (in a pattern similar to that observed with Kenton's body—although with deer and moose carcasses often much of the liver is consumed early on) and then the wolves rest nearby until the stomach empties sufficiently to allow for another feeding. Disarticulation of the prey carcass is not expected until sufficient flesh has been removed to allow this to occur with relative ease. At this point, the amount of edible flesh left on the carcass has decreased to the point where wolves are competing for what is left. Wolves respond by disarticulating the carcass and taking "their" piece to a safe location (in this case "safe" from their pack mates) to consume or chew on it. Thus, the fact that Kenton's body was not disarticulated by the 2–4 wolves (based on various witness accounts presented above from around the time of Kenton's death) in the area within a few hours of his having been killed is not surprising and certainly does not preclude involvement with wolves.

Similarly, although wolves often do not consume any of the contents of the stomachs of ungulates (deer, moose, caribou, elk, etc.) this should not be taken as evidence that wolves were not the primary predator feeding on Kenton's body. That wolves do not typically eat the contents of the stomachs of moose and deer (they certainly do eat the stomach tissue of these animals) is because a stomach full of chewed browse or fibrous herbaceous vegetation is not appealing to a predator such as a wolf. When wolves consume the carcasses of carnivores (I saw this with wolves feeding on wolf and wolverine carcasses used by Inuit hunters as bait in Nunavut), stomach contents are most often completely consumed. In short, whether wolves should be expected to consume the stomach contents of their prey is largely dependent on the diet of the prey in question. Although Kenton was a vegetarian, what he had for lunch on 8 November 2005 would have been much more palatable to wolves than the woody browse consumed by moose and elk at that time of year.

Kenton's body had flesh removed from the knees upward, and the stomach area was almost completely removed. Flesh was missing from his right arm, and portions of his right face were missing. We would expect a single feeding site if Kenton was killed by a single bear.

Patterson wrote,

I was struck by the overall pattern of feeding on Kenton's body. Although flesh was removed from the soft areas of the body from the knees to the chest, much muscle remained unconsumed on both thighs. This pattern of feeding in a relatively superficial manner over a large portion of the body, rather than focused feeding (i.e. all flesh consumed) over a more concentrated area, suggests multiple animals were feeding simultaneously (feeding over a larger area of the body). In contrast, in photos I have seen of a man consumed by grizzly bear, the flesh of the thighs was consumed down to the femur while many other areas of the body were untouched. I must state clearly though that I am no expert on the typical patterns of use of prey carcasses by either wolves or bears. More experienced experts should be consulted on these matters.

McNay's report included photographs of people killed and partially eaten by bears. The photos show concentrated feeding on only one area of the body, with the remainder of the body untouched.

THE TYPES OF INJURIES

Paquet and Walker claimed that "the large number of hae-morrhaged claw and bite wounds to Carnegie's head, face, and shoulders is a distinguishing characteristic of bear attacks on humans. From wolves, we expect to see fewer haemorrhaged wounds resulting from claws because their primary mode of attack is by biting. Claw wounds inflicted by wolves are secondary injuries that, based on our exam-ination of ungulate prey, often occur after death and show little haemorrhaging."

Whether a wound hemorrhages or not is very important. Hemorrhaged wounds occur only if inflicted upon a live sub-ject whose heart is still beating and pumping blood to the wound. Wounds that occur after death do not hemorrhage. Pathologists usually make note of any hemorrhaged wounds and detail them in their reports. Neither the necropsy report prepared by Walker (co-author of the report for the coroner) nor the preliminary anatomical diagnosis prepared by Dr. Brits mentions that any of the wounds was hemorrhaged. The closest either report comes to mentioning hemorrhaging is a short sentence by Walker: "The thyroid gland showed bleed-ing and lacerations."

I find this missing information in the reports a little strange. Having been defence counsel and later a Crown prosecutor involved in murder files, I have read many autopsy reports and have learned to pay close attention to whether a wound detailed in a report was hemorrhaged or not. I have come to expect that the pathologist preparing the report would mention that fact because it usually becomes important at trial.

Because hemorrhaging is not mentioned in the reports in this case, I can only assume that the evidence of its existence must come from either the photographs taken by Constable Noey at the scene or the photographs taken by Constable Tom Pack of the RCMP Forensic Identity Unit, who attended the autopsy and photographed it extensively. But to be fair, perhaps hemorrhaging was not noted during the autopsy precisely because this was not a murder investigation.

However, even if we accept that the wounds to the face were hemorrhaged and likely occurred at an early stage in the attack, this fact does not rule out wolves. In fact, it proves wolves. In 1984 at Key Lake, Jim Desroches was attacked by a wolf that went for his throat first. The initial attack on Fred Desjarlais in 2004 at Key Lake was also aimed at his throat. In 2016 at the Cigar Lake mine (which is between the Key Lake mine site and the Points North camp site), Bobby McCallum was attacked by a wolf that got its teeth into his throat and was holding him by the throat when a security guard intervened and chased the wolf away.

The suggestion by Paquet and Walker that "haemorrhaged claw and bite wounds to Carnegie's head, face, and shoulders is a distinguishing characteristic of bear attacks on humans," and not of attacks by wolves, is simply wrong. Wolves do attack the face and especially the throat, which might explain the bleeding and lacerations on Kenton's thyroid.

What might be typical of bears and not typical of wolves might be true over large numbers. But individual wolves and individual bears behave differently. There is a common saying that nineteen times out of twenty a black bear will run when it meets a human. It's that twentieth bear you have to be careful of.

When I was a kid there were still remnants of my father's dog team, a few dogs that my mother wanted to keep around after my father died. As children we played with them, and, being children, we played rough, and most of our play was pretend fighting. The dogs loved it. My mother didn't. We frequently came back in with our coat sleeves torn by dogs that had grabbed an arm during rough play. One of those dogs, a well-built husky type named Saber, was my dog exclusively, and I was the only one who would play fight with him. My brothers found it too unnerving because when Saber played at fighting he had a habit of going for your throat.

The claw marks on Kenton's face noted in the Paquet-Walker report were not extensive; they consisted of a furrow across the bridge of the nose, a deep cut along the left eyebrow, and minor scratches on the face. I have been scratched numerous times by playful sleigh dogs jumping up and raking their claws across an arm or bare patch of skin and even sometimes through a thin shirt. Even these playful accidental scratches can be deeper than the minor scratches that I observed on Kenton's face. At first, I suspected that the minor scratches on his face occurred while he was running away from the pursuing wolves and ran, blinded by terror, through tree branches. But when I put this theory to Noey, he didn't agree. He had followed Kenton's tracks and would have known whether he had run into tree branches. "No," he said. "The trees are too small and too far apart up there. It's more likely he received those scratches from shrubs while he was rolling around on the ground."

There are two deep parallel lacerations beginning at the hairline of Kenton's right forehead and extending toward the area above where his right ear had been. These lacerations do not look like claw marks. They are much too deep to have been made by a claw. And if they were made by a claw, the fact that there are only two of them would suggest that they were made by a wolf with two centre claws extending out beyond the other two claws rather than by a bear with its five almost parallel claws. If those two lacerations were made by a bear, judging by their depth, we would expect to find three more claw marks.

McNay addressed claw marks in his report:

As noted by Paquet and Walker (2006), black bears tend to attack the upper body, head and neck. Death can result from blows from the front paws that break the neck or back, or from bite wounds to the head and neck. Bruises with extensive shoulder and back injuries are frequent (Herrero 1985). Claw marks are common on the face, shoulders, back, and chest. Wolves may also bite the head and neck, but wolves do not use their feet in the process of grasping or killing prey so prominent claw marks would not be expected on a human killed by wolves. In my examination of RCMP Photos 931–933 and 942, I saw no marks on Kenton's body that would be definitive, or even suggestive, of bear claw marks.

Even if the initial attack on Kenton was not to the throat, cuts and scrapes to the head area do not necessarily indicate a bear. The photographs show that a large portion of Kenton's throat and the right side of his face, including his right ear, was eaten. It is more likely that the scrapes occurred as one of the wolves fed on his face while the others fed elsewhere on his body. I have seen sleigh dogs holding down a large piece of meat with one paw while tearing at it with their teeth. Any scrapes or claw marks to Kenton's head might be explained by this feeding characteristic—by the wolf holding the head down with a clawed paw and tearing at the right side of his face.

THE "SCIENTIFIC" CONSENSUS: IT WAS A BEAR

The problem with the Paquet-Walker report's assertion that "all outside experts who examined the evidence concluded independently that the most probable predator was a black bear" is that we are left to wonder which of the outside experts examined the evidence. Ontario Ministry of Natural Resources biologist Maria de Almeida was on the list of experts supposedly consulted. As noted earlier, she had a brief conversation with Paquet about public education, and during the course of their conversation Paquet mentioned evidence of the victim's clothes having been rolled back, and de Almeida discussed with him some of the bear fatalities in Ontario. She was never asked to review any evidence related to the case.

What Paquet told Dr. Patterson could not possibly have been true. He told Patterson during a phone conversation on October 10, 2006, that the predator that killed Kenton was strong enough to break his belt when the belt snagged on a stump while his body was being dragged. Kenton had not been wearing a belt. He was wearing nylon pants that did not have belt loops.

The assertion that *all* outside experts agreed is also false. Patterson did not agree. He was subsequently not included in the list of experts consulted for the Paquet-Walker report.

Dr. John Linnell, research scientist at the Norwegian Institute for Nature Research, in Trondheim, is included in the Paquet-Walker report's list of experts. In an email reply to Kenton's mother, Lori Carnegie, Linnell wrote,

> This reply is in haste—I am familiar with all the facts that you presented concerning the fact that he was definitely killed by wild animals (rather than some other form of accident or natural causes), the photographs being taken by other workers at a different location, the fact that he was not feeding wolves, the camp's dump and the habituation of wolves. The way that I understand it, the ongoing debate is mainly focused on the issues of if it was a bear, or a wolf who actually killed him? That was my reference to never really knowing what happened.
>
> I know about the captive wolf case—actually it is one of the few wolf attacks for which good forensic studies were conducted to reconstruct what actually happened. There is at least one scientific paper on this case. I also heard about the recent attack—but only through the media.
>
> As for Paul—I have met Paul once and have had a lot of email discussion with him over the years on many wolf topics. In connection with his involvement in the inquest surrounding this case we have exchanged emails—basically he has been asking if I have any more detailed information about wolf attacks than that which I included in "Fear of Wolves" report—and asking if I had any more contacts with people who might. I don't really know him that well personally—just on one hand he has been

involved in some good wolf science and that on the other he is a very vocal wolf advocate. I know there has been some discussion about how well he balances these two roles—but I really don't know enough to comment on this.

I contacted Linnell in August 2017. In an email reply to my questions—What evidence, if any, were you provided with to examine? Did you agree that the most probable predator was a black bear?—Linnell wrote,

> Paul discussed the case with me—describing what he knew, but mainly asking me if I had come across any good descriptions of how wolves "handled" humans that they had killed during my work to review the literature. I was not able to help, as the historic data did not cover such details, and most of the cases during more recent times have been kids/youths rather than adult males, plus no such details have been recorded. So, yes, I was an expert that he consulted. However, privately I never felt that there was enough evidence to conclude what had been involved, but as far as I remember I was not directly asked. Plus, I never saw all the evidence. Therefore, I was not among those experts who thought it was probably a bear.

Dr. Gary Haynes is listed as an expert in the Paquet-Walker report. He was involved in a National Geographic TV documentary that featured Paquet. In an email to Lori Carnegie, Haynes wrote,

> I am so sorry for the loss of your son.
> I don't think I had any kind of role in the official investigation. My association with the case was limited to the

filming of the TV documentary. I was asked to appear on film by National Geographic TV as a scientist with experiences in examining wolf-prey interactions. I was filmed one day at Points North talking with the local coroner and thinking out loud about commonalities in wolf behavior. I was never asked to speak with a medical examiner, the police or any court officials. The information that I knew of the death is repeated on the TV episode, and I basically agreed onscreen that your son must have been attacked by wild animals while he was out walking by himself. My other function in the program was to examine the open dump that drew animals to the outskirts of the Points North depot, and to decry the potential danger it was creating.

This case is not the first I've been associated with through National Geographic TV, but it certainly has made a deep and lasting impact on me. I spent many days alone in wolf country in the 1980s, and sometimes I was very nervous (because I was always unarmed and wolves and bears occasionally were very close to me). In the program, it appears that one possible conclusion could be that your son was killed by a black bear, and that wolves may not necessarily be to blame. I always felt strongly threatened by bears but not so much by the wolves I was studying— and now I have to wonder if maybe I was lucky to have survived those years in the field.

I am sorry for the death of your son, and I don't think I'll ever forget this case. I don't know if I have answered your questions—please let me know.

Lori Carnegie took Haynes up on his request that she let him know if he had or hadn't answered her questions. She sent a subsequent email with the following questions:

Who approached you on behalf of National Geographic and what dates were you involved?

Do you believe the dump is relevant in relation to the habituation of wolves?

Do you believe they [wolves] could attack a human?

What evidence were you shown to support the possibility of a black bear attack?

Were you shown photographs of the scene and my son's body?

Did you have an opportunity to speak with Dr. Paul Paquet while on this assignment?

Haynes replied to Lori, stating in part, "When I arrived, I did speak with Paul Paquet who told me about the investigation that was going on. He filled me in on the known circumstances of the case, such as the time when your son took his walk and the discovery of his death later that evening....I was sent photos by email to answer specific queries, such as the views of the spot where the body was located, animal tracks in the snow, and views of the lake and depot, which were shown on TV episode."

In another email to Lori Carnegie, Haynes wrote, "I am not a good source of information about the details of the death scene, since I didn't see all the evidence collected there. The information I was given was useful but I wished there had been more finer details."

So, while Haynes had access to more of the evidence than some of the other listed experts, it seems he did not have all of the evidence. But even after reviewing the evidence that he was provided with, Haynes denied that he agreed that it was most likely a bear. Further on in the email to Lori quoted above, he wrote, "The interpretation of bear involvement came from a bear expert, not from me. That's about all I can tell you, since I wasn't involved in the more detailed judicial proceedings."

There was no bear expert involved. Crichton was a moose expert, not a bear expert.

Most striking is the omission of McNay from the list of experts. In support of McNay's inclusion, Patterson wrote,

> Finally, although there is much less precedence for drawing inference on wolf-human encounters due to relative scarcity of attacks, Mark McNay, of Alaska Fish and Game, has reviewed the available information more thoroughly than anyone else in North America and has published 2 peer-reviewed scientific papers dealing with wolf attacks on people. He should have been heavily consulted, if not directly involved, in this investigation.

In addition to the two papers mentioned by Patterson (see bibliography), McNay wrote a third, more detailed technical bulletin about wolf-human interactions, titled "A Case History of Wolf-Human Encounters in Alaska and Canada." Though not peer reviewed, it details eighty such encounters. In its introduction, McNay states,

> Previous reviews of wolf-human interactions found that wolf aggression toward humans was rare in North America (Young 1944; Rutter and Pimlott 1968; Mech 1970, 1990). Those reviews discounted most descriptions of wolf aggression as either exaggerations or as misinterpretations of benign encounters. When wolf attacks were substantiated, in both Europe and North America, most were attributed to either rabid wolves or to wolf-dog hybrids (Rutter and

Pimlott 1968; Mech 1970). Consequently, it is now widely accepted among biologists that healthy, wild wolves present little threat to people....

However, in April 2000 a wolf attacked and repeatedly bit a 6-year-old boy near Icy Bay, Alaska. That incident stimulated a debate in the Alaskan legislature that questioned the generally accepted view of wolf-human interactions. Wolf control was proposed for some rural areas to enhance public safety, and biologists were unable to add scientific perspective to the debate because there was no recent compilation of records that documented wolf aggression toward people in North America.

Following the incident in Icy Bay, I began to solicit and compile cases of wolf-human encounters in which wolf behavioural responses to human presence deviated from what was considered "normal" avoidance. I did not limit my investigation to aggressive encounters but included cases where wolves displayed nonaggressive, yet fearless, behavior. The case history presented here is the culmination of that investigation. The purpose of this technical bulletin is to provide a current perspective for wolf-human interactions in a variety of contexts in Alaska and Canada.

McNay's technical bulletin includes forty-one cases from provinces and territories in Canada, thirty-six cases that occurred in Alaska; and three cases that occurred in northern Minnesota. Of these eighty cases, thirty-nine contained elements of aggression by healthy wolves, twenty-nine were non-aggressive encounters, and twelve involved known or suspected rabid wolves. In sixteen cases, healthy wolves bit people or bit into their clothing; most bites were minor. Severe bites occurred in six incidents, four of which involved children—none of these severe bites was life threatening, although the injuries to the children could have been more serious if rescuers had not intervened. Six cases involved aggression by wolves toward people who were accompanied by dogs, and in two of those cases the wolves bit people.

No other expert listed in the appendix to the Paquet-Walker report has done nearly as much research specifically on wolf-human interactions in North America than McNay. His exclusion speaks volumes. It seems the report's authors did not want to admit that wolves attack people, even if those attacks are rare.

Valerius Geist, professor emeritus of environmental science at the University of Calgary, had the opportunity to review the evidence pertaining to the attack on Kenton Carnegie. The information was provided to him by the Carnegie family. He subsequently wrote a brief report, which concluded, "As to Kenton Joel Carnegie's tragic death I harbor no doubts. He was killed and consumed by wolves."

Geist worked at the same university as Paquet. The reason Geist was not consulted might be because his view of wolves is apparently contrary to Paquet's. A 2007 draft of Geist's paper "When Do Wolves Become Dangerous to Humans?" tackles the romantic view of wolves. In it, Geist disagrees with "the politically correct view of wolves, currently vehemently and dogmatically defended,...that wolves are 'harmless' and of no danger to humans." In this draft he examines how science about wolves became slanted in North American literature about wolves, suggesting that the scientists "were greatly aided in this by premature conclusions about free-living and captive wolves, as well [as] by a brilliant literary prank by a renowned Canadian author and humorist, which illustrated wolves as harmless mouse eaters."

BUT...BEARS WERE HIBERNATING

Completely ignored in the Paquet-Walker report in coming to the conclusion that "the preponderance of indirect evidence suggests Carnegie was attacked and killed by a black bear rather than by wolves" is the fact that black bears hibernate, and this attack occurred in November, when bears are normally asleep.

McNay has identified denning dates in a variety of northern continental climates, including Lake Nipissing, Ontario; Cold Lake, Alberta; and Yukon River, Alaska. The latitude of Points North camp is 58 degrees, 15 minutes north. McNay estimated the mean denning date for black bears at this latitude as October 13. He estimated the latest date that a bear should be out and about at the Points North camp as October 27—a full twelve days before the attack on Kenton Carnegie.

Snow had begun to accumulate in mid-October 2005, and the lake was frozen thick enough for a person to walk on. Bear food such as berries, insects, vegetation, carrion, and small mammals would have been difficult to find. Weather information indicates that the minimum temperature had consistently been below freezing on all but two nights between the middle of October and the fateful day of November 8. It had snowed on November 5 and 6. This new snow cover over the little snow that had already been there made tracking much easier.

McNay's research on denning dates shows patterns—but reality doesn't always obey the rules, and sometimes bears will stay out later if there is food for them. Given the weather conditions and that a bear's normal food would have been absent or covered by snow, the only place for a bear to find sustenance would have been at the garbage dump near the Points North camp.

However, no one at the Points North camp had seen a bear or any tracks or any other indication of a bear during this time frame, neither near the camp nor at the garbage dump, nor on any roads in the vicinity. The last sighting of a bear at the Points North camp prior to the attack on Kenton was in late summer, when a bear was shot and killed near the camp kitchen. Nor were any bears or tracks of bears seen after the attack on Kenton.

Tim Trottier, a SERM biologist, was in Points North in late September 2005, more than a month prior, and during the night saw a bear through the window of the room he was staying in. Trottier is one of the experts listed in the Paquet-Walker report.

REVISITING THE INVESTIGATION

A central theme of the Paquet-Walker report is that the first investigators on the scene were not experts and messed things up.

Although Constable Noey originally reported sighting 2 wolves while searching for the body, his report does not mention animal tracks, faecal material, urine marks, or hair as having been found around the body or along the drag path....

[P]hotographs taken at the scene the same day by Noey show tracks of black bear and smaller animals, likely foxes. Although the age of the tracks in the photographs cannot be determined, the failure to report their presence suggests a predetermined focus on wolves, an oversight in reporting, or inexperience in identifying tracks.

The authors continue on the following pages of their report:

Although knowledge and skill are often necessary to determine the cause of injuries or death resulting from predation, there is a logical, systematic procedure for evaluating predator kills and feeding....With sufficient care and evaluation of indirect evidence, ruling out or confirming the responsible predator with a reasonable degree of certainty is often possible....

No feces, urine marks, hair, or bedsites were documented or collected, although we doubt searchers and investigators were cognizant of the significance of these signs and therefore might have ignored them....Although quite prominent in the photographs, bear tracks were not mentioned in the RCMP report detailing examination of the accident scene. We believe this was an oversight owing to inexperience in identifying tracks of wild animals.

Paquet and Walker end their report with this paragraph:

Predator sign is often found near kill sites. Where predation is suspected or confirmed, locate and document the site of the attack, body of the victim, and feeding sites if possible. Avoid tracking over or destroying evidence such as tracks and droppings around these sites and the body. Search the area surrounding the body thoroughly for tracks, scat, urine marks, bed sites, and drag marks. Collect and freeze hair, scat, and urine. Examine the body for wounds, haemorrhages, bruises, broken bones, and feeding. Because feeding and other predator sign may be similar, having all available evidence is essential to confirm the cause of death and/or the species responsible. Finally, make as few assumptions as possible and reserve judgement until assumptions have been eliminated or vindicated, i.e. no presuppositions.

The report's authors assert that the initial investigators did not follow the correct protocol for investigating a predatory attack. But there had not been a previously confirmed wild wolf kill of a human in North America in nearly a century. There simply was no established protocol to follow.

The initial investigators did everything they knew to preserve the site. Upon first finding the body, Eikel, Van Galder, and Svarckopf did not approach it. Two of them didn't even look at it. When Eikel and Burseth returned to confirm what had initially been seen, they also did not approach the body. They viewed it from a distance and stayed only long enough to confirm what they needed to know.

No one else approached the site until Constable Noey and coroner Rosalie Tsannie-Burseth arrived. Upon their arrival, Tsannie-Burseth, her husband, and Eikel were instructed to walk single file behind Noey so as not to make unnecessary footprints. Upon finding the body, they did what they needed to do. Noey photographed the body and the scene, taking thirty distinct photographs. The photographs are all of good quality and depict the scene and the body clearly, including the stump that Kenton's pants were caught on. Noey and Burseth then bagged the body.

Noey made notes detailing the wolf tracks he saw, describing the two wolves he saw near the body, and stating that he fired two shotgun blasts into the air to scare the wolves away.

Noey instructed Eikel, the camp manager, not to allow anyone in to the scene before he had a chance to investigate the next day in daylight. No one went close to the scene until Noey returned the next day when it was possible to see.

The only tracks made by humans before Noey returned the next day to photograph the scene were on the trail that follows the shore of the lake. Eikel, Van Galder, and Svarckopf followed Kenton's tracks along the trail and turned back when they noted his tracks had turned back. They did not follow his tracks all the way to where he had stood on the shore of the lake (point 3 on Noey's map). Eikel and Burseth followed the same trail when they returned and stayed on the trail while they viewed the body. The evidence of wolves around the initial site, the drag zone, and the final site was not disturbed before Noey arrived and photographed those sites.

Paquet and Walker suggest that a predetermined focus upon wolves had slanted the investigation away from the bear. Yet this focus on wolves likely resulted from two factors: the only tracks any of the searchers recognized were wolf tracks, and there were at least two wolves at the body when Noey and Tsannie-Burseth arrived.

The suggestion that they were inexperienced trackers because they failed to see bear tracks is self-serving. There were no bear tracks. The only person who claimed to see bear tracks in the photos was Crichton, who also told Lori Carnegie that he saw *no wolf tracks* in the photographs he examined. Crichton was a moose biologist who incidentally saw bear tracks near where moose had been killed. Bear tracks are so different from wolf tracks that a person need not be an "expert" to recognize the difference. If there had been bear tracks in the area, they would have been quite noticeable to

REVISITING THE INVESTIGATION   105

Noey and Tsannie-Burseth, both of whom searched the area looking specifically at tracks.

Conservation officers Kelly Crane and Mario Gaudet reported, "Officers investigated the site and found numerous wolf tracks in the area. No other large animal tracks could be found." They too looked specifically at the tracks.

Burseth and Eikel reported seeing only wolf tracks. Burseth, who had been in the area for seventeen years, knew the difference between wolf and bear tracks. Yet Paquet and Walker consistently state throughout their report that bear tracks were found at the site, based solely on Crichton's opinion. They use this presumed fact to discredit the people who saw only wolf tracks.

The suggestion by the report's authors that the initial investigation was flawed because no one picked up scat, hair, or urine samples supposes that there was scat, hair, or urine to be collected. Noey photographed the area in detail, especially the area around the initial site where the body was found and the drag marks from that site to the body's final position. No scat, hair, or urine marks can be seen in any of the photographs.

I specifically asked Noey about scat and hair when I interviewed him. He said there was none, and if there had been any, he would have photographed it. Keep in mind that Noey was a trained police officer investigating a sudden death. Scat, hair, or bed sites would have fit into the category of evidence he was gathering.

Bear scat is typically very large and obvious. It is often in a pile thirty centimetres in diameter and up to fifteen centimetres high. It is hard not to see. If Noey had seen bear scat in the area that he photographed, he would have noted it. It's not something a police officer intent upon documenting a scene in as much detail as possible would have ignored.

Fresh wolf scat is not as pronounced as bear scat, but it too would have been obvious to Noey and Tsannie-Burseth as they searched the area for evidence. The two conservation officers, Crane and Gaudet, also searched the area. They did not report finding any scat, hair, or urine marks. That the searchers did not find any scat, hair, or urine marks is probably because there was none to find rather than, as suggested by the report writers, because they lacked experience or expertise.

The report strongly suggests that the investigation was flawed because it was not conducted by experts. Yet the supposed expert who identified bear tracks at the scene has been completely discredited.

The idea that we will never know for certain what happened to Kenton Carnegie because the initial investigation was flawed permeates the literature that followed the incident. For example, in a book chapter titled "Predators that Kill Humans: Myth, Reality, Context and the Politics of Wolf Attacks on People," authors John D.C. Linnell and Julien Alleau state, "Until 2005, none of these attacks had been fatal. However, an adult man was killed at a remote mining exploration site in northern Saskatchewan in November 2005 (McNay 2007). It was clear from the site that he had been killed by a large predator, but the crime scene investigation and autopsy were not handled very efficiently leading to some doubt as to the predator species responsible."

In my opinion, the only confusion about the investigation or the autopsy comes from the deliberate attempt by the report's writers to create confusion. Their suggestion that the investigation was flawed supported their conclusion that the most likely attacker was a black bear. The only way the authors could assert their conclusion was to discredit everyone who concluded otherwise.

Science is important. It is with good science that we learn about our environment and our role in that environment. I acknowledge that pure objective science is difficult and that every scientist will have subjective biases that will slant their work. But it is expected that a real scientist knows their own bias and guards against it. That doesn't seem to be what happened here. It seems the authors of this report deliberately slanted the evidence in an apparent attempt to deflect negative attention from wolves.

Yes, in past decades, steps were taken to eradicate wolves based on a misunderstanding of the wolf's role in ecology. Yes, unreasonable fear of wolves contributed to the problem. But we don't cure a misunderstanding, or alleviate fear, by deliberately slanting a public report in the other direction. That simply discredits all scientists in the eyes of the public.

OTHER EXPLANATIONS

MY THOUGHTS ON WOLVES

The one thing I learned from my encounter with the wolf that morning in 1986, more than anything else, is that humans are not special. We are not God's chosen creatures. We can be food in the chain and nothing more.

Every living thing on the planet has three commandments: eat, don't be eaten, and procreate. All I was doing that morning was obeying my commandment to not be eaten. The wolf was obeying his commandment to eat. We were equals, neither of us superior or inferior in any way.

Prior to the encounter, I had read Farley Mowat's book *Never Cry Wolf*. I had believed the silly notion that wolves do not attack humans. There is no basis for this belief. It's completely irrational. Humans and wolves are the top predators in this ecological zone. The reason the wolf usually doesn't attack us is not because God likes us or that there is a covenant of some sort between humans and wolves. The wolf has learned to avoid us because we are dangerous animals. We are unnatural. We have all sorts of smells that are generally not found in nature: the smell of petroleum, of iron, of smoke, of perfumes. We don't smell like normal food; we smell like something outside of the wolf's world.

I hold no animosity toward the wolf that regarded me only as meat. I saw his abilities, how fast he could move, how he did everything without a wasted motion. He didn't growl or snarl or in any way vocalize, out of pure efficiency. Those actions would be wasted energy. Canine growls and snarls are the way the animal communicates an intention: *Come any closer and I will bite you* or *Get out of my territory*. A growl is an intimidation. It is meant as a warning or a threat. The wolf that morning had no reason to warn or threaten me—indeed, to do so would have been counter to his intention. There is no need to threaten or warn food.

I respect his incredible abilities, his physical prowess, his capacity for survival, his intellect, and even his spirit. The only reason I survived that morning and did not become his breakfast is that the wolf did not know how pathetically weak and slow I was in comparison to him. I survived because I bluffed and the wolf didn't call me on my bluff.

When I got home after my week at work, I went to ask my mother about wolves. She was born in 1921 at Big Trout Lake, in what would later become Prince Albert National Park. Her father was a trapper and fisherman. She had married a trapper and fisherman, and when her husband died of a heart attack and left her with six children to support, she became a trapper and fisherwoman. She should know something about wolves.

When I asked if she had ever heard of wolves attacking humans, she replied, "Of course. Your great uncles 'Dolphus and Zacchaeus spent a night up a tree and watched while a pack of wolves ate their dog team. They had a .22 with them and shot wolves throughout the night. In the morning after the pack left, there were no dead wolves. They had taken their dead away with them."

Her telling that story brought back memories of when I was about ten or twelve years old and on the trapline with her. We sometimes saw wolf tracks on top of the footprints we had left the day before, indicating that the wolf had been tracking us. Mom wasn't afraid, but she did warn us kids to be careful.

There are people in our society who hold a romantic view of wolves, and they are likely going to be concerned that I am writing about wolves attacking people. The romanticized view says that wolves are special, majestic, spiritual animals that can do no wrong.

I disagree that wolves are in any way special. They exist in this ecosystem equally with all the elements of the forest, from bacteria that fuel plant growth to the mice and rabbits and deer and moose that eat the plants. The wolf is no more special than the other carnivores: the owl or the lynx or the mink or the wolverine, each of which has physical attributes comparable to, and in cases superior to, the wolf. The mink is not only a sleek land hunter; it also goes into the water, as does its cousin the otter. The lynx's ability to run on top of the snow is superior to that of the wolf, and it is equally intelligent, curious, and capable. For sheer physical prowess, it is difficult to think of any animal superior to the wolverine. Built low to the ground, all muscle and claws and teeth, it has earned the respect of northern trappers.

I agree that a wolf is a majestic creature. The one that attacked me was very impressive aesthetically and physically. It was pure black with silver flecks on its sides. It moved with speed and grace and efficiency of motion that a martial artist or a dancer would do well to study.

I even agree that a wolf can do no wrong—because in his world there is no right and wrong. In his world, you either survive or you don't. He has no room for moral judgments. The wolf I encountered wasn't breaking any rules of behaviour.

He was acting according to the basic instinctual code he was born with, a code that does not rank animals in terms of being special.

Is the wolf a spiritual animal?

He is certainly well known and respected in Cree culture. He is often associated with the Eagle, the Bear, and the Buffalo as one of the spirit helpers. But this view can be misleading. The four animals are not the only spirit helpers but merely the ones that get the most attention. The woodpecker, the mouse, the butterfly, and the dragonfly are also special spirit helpers. Any animal, and even plants, can become a familiar to an animist. If we follow this traditional line of reasoning, we have to keep in mind that humans in this tradition are also spirit animals. The notion that a wolf deserves to be respected because it has a spirit is true for all four-legged animals, for the flying nation of birds, for the insect nation, for the swimming nation of fish (who know the most about the life-giving power of water), for the standing nation of trees, for the nation of plants that provide us with medicine, and for the nation of two-legged animals, the humans. We are all spirit beings occupying Turtle Island, and we all deserve to be treated with respect.

The concern of the romantics is well founded. They worry that people are going to go out and kill the wolves. This fear is based upon very real historical experience. Humans, especially in North America, have in the past decimated the wolf population.

Contrary to the romantics are the gun people who believe that their view is pragmatic. They want to shoot any wolf that might come around because wolves are dangerous predators that might eat cattle or pets—especially if it is shown that wolves attack humans.

A few years ago, the gun lobby in Saskatchewan sought a bounty on coyotes. They argued that the province's coyote population was out of control and that the coyotes were killing sheep and calves. They made ecological arguments to justify their request. They said that when the coyote population got too high, mange would break out and coyotes would suffer. So they wanted a bounty on coyotes: first, to protect livestock; and second, because they were concerned about the health of the coyotes. Interestingly, even though mange became a major theme in the lobby—with people phoning in to radio stations and describing the horrifying deaths of animals that had lost most of their fur and slowly, painfully frozen to death—no one had seen a coyote with mange at the time of the lobby.

They got their bounty and went out and slaughtered coyotes. Two years later the gun people were back. This time they wanted a bounty on gophers because the gopher population was out of control. In this second lobbying effort, they did not mention that the surge in the gopher population was due to a lack of coyotes. The coyotes they had shot two winters before had kept the gopher population in check.

The truth is that gun people want an excuse to shoot their guns. They want to kill wolves and coyotes and gophers, not entirely for pragmatic reasons, such as protection of life and property, but primarily because shooting a gun is exciting to them. They would love for the government to give them permission to carry handguns when they are out in the forest to protect themselves from the proven-dangerous wolf. Anything less, they would argue, is irresponsible.

To the gun people who want to use my discourse on wolves as a justification for greater armament, or maybe even bounties on wolves, I would reply with the observation that in

North America more people are killed and injured by their own children than by wolves. They have more reason to carry handguns to protect themselves from their sons and daughters and grandchildren than to protect themselves from wolves.

I sympathize with the wolf at another level as well. I know what it feels like to be discriminated against based on false stories. The story of the savage, uneducated, backward Indian has parallels with the story of the rabid killer wolf. The romantic story of the Indian as stoic mystic is analogous to the romantic story of the mysterious spirit wolf. These racist stories about us and the unbalanced stories about the wolf have resulted in both Indigenous Peoples and the wolf being neither understood nor fully appreciated.

The American Indian has been romanticized by those who see us as mystical and stoic. J.K. Rowling, the author of the Harry Potter series, has tried to cash in on American Indian traditional knowledge. In "History of Magic in North America," a series of online essays, Rowling attempts to tell the stories of "wandless magic" and "skin walkers" without understanding the contexts of those stories. She attempts to compare medicine men with wizards from her Eurocentric mythology and, in my view, fails miserably. A medicine man is not a wizard. His work with plants is not potion making. It is medicine making. He doesn't cast spells. He doesn't command mystical forces. Instead, a medicine man is one who can ask those forces to help—and they might help, if they are so inclined, or they might not.

The negative stories of Indigenous Peoples tell of our brutality, how we scalped innocent pioneers and tortured priests. The stories of our sadistic skill in inflicting pain upon any white man or woman taken prisoner are as well known as the stories about our medicine men. The words *savage* and *savagery* come from these stories. The original French word *sauvage* meant wild or unspoiled. It has come to mean nasty, brutish, and cruel.

Parallel stories, two stories that are both true at the same time, can be a difficult concept to accept. The twin stories of Indigenous Peoples as environmental stewards in tune with and connected to the land and as struggling with poverty and survival in inner-city ghettos and underfunded reservations are both true.

The story of the wolf as a misunderstood, unfairly perse-cuted, beautiful animal is as true as the story of the wolf as the killer of cattle and wildlife. The wolf was killed indiscrim-inately, governments did pay bounties, he was poisoned, and a concerted effort was made to eradicate him. And the wolf will take a calf or a stray sheep and will attack humans.

THE WOLF IN CREE TRICKSTER STORIES

The Cree have a rich tradition of storytelling. Our genesis sto-ries tell of our first ancestors being lowered on a web by Spider from a place above and of how Bear was the first animal to take pity on them and teach them. He taught us humans many things, but we abused his teachings, so he did not give us the ultimate teaching: he did not teach us how to hibernate.

The saga that contains the richest storytelling is about the early life of Wesakicahk, also known as the Trickster. He was the first son of the first people, at a time when there was still much magic and the humans and the animals could still communicate with each other.

His parents had a rather nasty falling out, with his father ultimately chopping off his mother's head. His father then fled back to the sky and sought the protection of his father, the star Polaris. Wesakicahk's mother—now in two parts: a head and a body—directed the body to chase her murderer into the sky, and there they are to this day. Wesakicahk's father is the big dipper circling Polaris, and the body of his wife is the little dipper, perpetually chasing him.

The head was extremely enraged and determined to get revenge on the man by killing his sons, even though they were her sons as well. The two boys were warned by their father before he left that she would do this. He gave the oldest son, Wesakicahk, four pieces of magic to protect himself with and told him to look after his brother.

The saga tells of Wesakicahk's flight, carrying his little brother on his back with his famous mother, the Rolling Head, chasing them. It's a rather gruesome story filled with images of an angry rolling head, torn by thorns and singed by fire, all covered in blood and dirt and soot.

The sons eventually escape but are alone in the world. The little brother, Mahigan, cries inconsolably, and Wesakicahk makes a ball out of strips of willow bark wound together. While he is playing with his little brother, trying to cheer him up, the ball goes into the lake.

An evil person arrives in a magic canoe that only needs the evil person to bang on its side to command it to go. This evil person slyly offers to help the boys get their ball back. He extends his paddle to the shore and tells Wesakicahk to stand on it, and he will take him to his ball. Wesakicahk is tricked and ends up dumped into the canoe. The evil person bangs on the side of the canoe, and the canoe leaves. Mahigan is left alone on the shore. He cries so hard at his loss, wailing from his loneliness, that he becomes a wolf.

As he is being kidnapped, Wesakicahk yells back at his brother, telling him to not be afraid, that he will come back for him, and warning him not to go anywhere near water. Mahigan yells back that it's okay because now he is a wolf and can look after himself.

Wesakicahk has several more adventures, ultimately defeating the evil person with skill and magic, but he is kept busy for a long time—maybe in part because he married the evil person's third daughter. Eventually Wesakicahk frees himself from the evil person, and we never again hear about that particular wife. He goes searching for his little brother.

Mahigan remembered his older brother's warning about water and usually stayed well clear of it. But one day, true to his wolf nature, while chasing a deer that went into the water, Mahigan followed it in. He was immediately captured by the water cats, who dragged him under.

Wesakicahk found his brother's footprints and followed them until they came to a lake. On the shore was Kingfisher, looking into the water. Wesakicahk asked the bird what it was looking at, and Kingfisher replied, "The water cats. They are playing with the hide they took from your brother, Mahigan, after they killed him."

Kingfisher helped Wesakicahk to trick the water cats. In the end, all the water cats were dead, and Wesakicahk had brought his little brother back to life. But in killing the powerful water cats, Wesakicahk caused a great flood that covered the entire world.

Wesakicahk, in a canoe with all of the animals he has saved, sent Muskrat down to find land after Otter and Beaver had failed. Muskrat almost died but finally succeeded in bringing up a little dirt in its paw. Wesakicahk used that little bit of dirt to recreate Turtle Island. He blew on it, and every time he blew, the dirt became larger and larger. Beaver used his tail to flatten the land, and eventually they had something they thought might be big enough. Wesakicahk asked Mahigan to go and check. Mahigan was gone half a day, and when he came back he said it wasn't big enough yet. So Wesakicahk blew on it some more. Again Mahigan went out and came back after a day and said it still wasn't big enough. So Wesakicahk blew on it again. And again Mahigan went out to check. This time he never came back, and that was how Wesakicahk knew Turtle Island was large enough.

This is a very abbreviated version of multiple sagas that tell of how we got here and how we learned to live on this planet. Wesakicahk eventually becomes known as the Trickster and is a central character in the sagas. From him we learn that everything is not the way it might seem, that there is good and bad in everything, and that good and bad might be the same thing.

About twenty years ago I stopped in to see an old friend named Rod McDermott. In the course of visiting I told a traditional Wesakicahk story. The old man then told me the follow-up story to the one I had told. I had never heard the follow-up. He then told me stories for a day and a half. One of those stories was about how humans got dogs:

Kayas, Wesakicahk went to the animals and told them that the two-leggeds, the humans, were having a hard time and needed help. He told the animals that whoever went to help the two-leggeds would be well looked after by them. He said in order to decide who gets to live with them and help them, the animals should have a race, and the winner of the race would be the one chosen.

So the animals lined up. There was Wolf and Dog and Coyote and Fox. Right off the start, Fox was in the lead, but he soon tired and dropped back. Then Coyote got tired and dropped back. Near the end there was Wolf in the lead with Dog right behind him. Dog had a strong heart and lungs, but he was having trouble keeping up with Wolf. They came over a hill and could see the two-leggeds' camp in the valley below. The race was almost over, and Wolf was sure to win. But just then a deer ran across in front of them, and Wolf could not resist chasing it. So that is how we got Dog as our helper. We have a promise, made by Wesakicahk on our behalf, to take good care of him. But imagine what it might have been like if that deer hadn't distracted Wolf.

Wesakicahk is a complex character with many faces. He fits well within a discussion of parallel stories. He was around at the beginning and fits in the Cree genesis stories, but there are the other stories too. We have to keep in mind that he is above all the Trickster, and no matter how we think of him the opposite is also true. He teaches how to be and equally how not to be. The following story tells of his less admirable side.

Kayas, Wesakicahk was poor and pitiful. A Frenchman came among the people trading with the Cree for animal pelts. Wesakicahk decided he too wanted some of the finery the trader had brought. He went to him and said, "I want two pairs of trousers, two blankets, two shirts and a gun, and I will bring you all kinds of fur."

The trader agreed and gave Wesakicahk the items he had asked for. Wesakicahk went home and showed his wife all that he had bargained for. His wife laughed at him. "How are you going to pay for all this? You're not a trapper. You don't even know how to trap."

Wesakicahk went back to the trader and said, "I need poison. Give me poison and I will bring you all kinds of wolf

and fox pelts." The trader agreed and gave Wesakicahk
strychnine. He took it home and told his wife to bring him
fat, all the fat she could find. He took the fat and melted it
down and added the poison to it. Then when the fat cooled
he made it into little balls. Then he went to the forest looking for wolves.

When he found a wolf, the wolf wouldn't come close to
him. Wesakicahk said, "Don't be afraid, my little brother.
I am not here to kill you. I have brought a great gift for the
wolf nation."

The wolf was still cautious. Wesakicahk told it, "Go and
tell all the wolves to come, and ask all the good-looking
foxes to come too. I want to preach to you."

The wolf did as Wesakicahk asked and brought all his
relatives and all the foxes, especially the foxes that were
handsome. When they gathered, Wesakicahk told them to
sit in a circle and said he was going to preach to them. The
wolves did as he asked, sitting in a large circle along with
all the foxes.

Wesakicahk began to preach to them. He told them to
be good and obedient wolves and foxes and that it was
important that they learned to do as they were told and
to not question things. They should believe what he said
because he said it.

Then he told them he was going to give them all a bless-
ing and told them to close their eyes and open their mouths.
The wolves and foxes did as they were told because they
wanted to be good and obedient wolves and foxes. Then
Wesakicahk went around and put a little ball of fat on each
of their tongues.

When he was done, he told them they could open their
eyes. But none of them did because they were all dead. He

skinned all those wolves and good-looking foxes and took their coats and gave those coats to the trader.

MY OWN FURTHER EXPERIENCES WITH WOLVES

I've encountered a few wolves since my first experience at the Key Lake mine in 1986 and the Carnegie inquest. One I would like to relate occurred here at my cabin a few years ago. I was out front early in the morning, welcoming the new day. As I came back to the cabin, the front of which is made entirely of glass, I saw the reflection of a wolf behind me. I turned, and he was on the lake ice about a hundred metres away. I told him in a very loud voice, "Get the fuck away from here. I don't want you around bothering my dogs." The wolf trotted north about another hundred metres, stopped, and looked back. I told him again, "Keep fucking going." He did, and I haven't seen a wolf so close to the cabin again.

I encountered another wolf about a kilometre from the cabin a few years later. This one was swimming across the river. I and my nephew were in a boat. It was a cold, snowy, and wet late-October afternoon. Upon approaching the animal, my nephew said, "Uncle, I think one of your dogs got loose." My original intention was to drive up to it and ask my nephew to grab it and pull it into the boat, but first I wanted to see which of my dogs had gotten loose.

I do have a dog named Bob that I have seen fishing. Another early morning out front of the cabin, something was swimming beyond the dock. It wasn't a beaver, because it had ears. I watched while it swam in circles for a while, and then it came to shore, and I couldn't see it because it was on the other side of the dock. When Bob came up on the shore he was carrying a pike that, judging by its size, must have weighed about ten pounds. I really doubt Bob caught it. More likely it was floating dead as sometimes happens when the water in July is very warm.

The animal swimming across the river that I and my nephew came across was not Bob, even though it was similar in size and colouring, tan and white. We circled the wolf with the boat, kept it out in the water away from the shore. It would have been no problem to keep circling it until it drowned. But what would have been the point of that? It still had its summer coat, and its pelt would not be prime. And even if it was prime and fit for sale, it would at best be worth only about two hundred dollars. Certainly not enough for me to kill an animal that has much more value in the wild. We left it to continue its journey. It wasn't near enough to where I live for me to admonish it for coming too close.

From where my wife Joan and I park our vehicles to the cabin is about two and a half kilometres. It's a nice walk in the winter. We have frequently seen fresh wolf tracks on that trail. It's unnerving to be walking home and looking down on fresh tracks that were made between the time I left that morning and my return and that are headed toward the cabin and my dogs. Wolves eat dogs, and I have had a dog taken off her chain by a wolf.

I have tracked wolves on that trail several times, and each time the tracks come within two hundred metres of the cabin and then abruptly veer either north or south and detour around my home and my dogs.

Incidentally, the dog that was taken was named Pithisew. She had been troublesome since I got her. She was prone to picking fights and would not get along with her team mates. She was one of the few dogs I have kept that I could not make friends with. She bred with my best sleigh dog and produced a litter of pups, all of which she killed and ate. As far as I am concerned, the wolf that came, killed her, and broke her chain when he dragged her away did me a favour.

WE DON'T KNOW IF WE DON'T STUDY

A person would think that after Kenton Joel Carnegie was killed, and a coroner's jury determined that he was killed by wolves and that this was the first documented case of wolves killing a human in North America in over a hundred years, the government would be motivated to study wolves. However, that did not happen.

It's confusing. It seems the government doesn't want to know. It's not conservativism versus liberalism. Both styles of government are equally wilfully blind.

I am a commercial fisher on Montreal Lake, as were my father and my grandfather. In 2005 the fishers here noticed that something was wrong with our lake. People with a life-time of fishing experience couldn't find the walleye. They had suddenly disappeared. We called in the government and demanded that our lake be closed to all fishing until we figured out what was going on. The government agreed that we could stop commercial fishing but insisted that the sport fishers be allowed to continue to take fish, though at a reduced limit. The problem with limits on recreational fishers is that no one monitors them. But at the same time, with no walleye here, the sport fishers stayed away.

We tried to figure out what had happened. Was it acid rain from Fort McMurray? We are on the downwind side of the tar sands. The acidity of Montreal Lake is up slightly but not enough to account for the sudden, drastic change.

Was it loss of spawning sites? With the extremely low price for beaver pelts, there were very few trappers, and beaver had dammed many of the creeks the walleye used for spawning.

We finally found out what had happened and who was responsible. We were. We had overfished our lake. Walleye might not have the greatest taste, but they do bring the best price. Our American neighbours love them. If you put enough batter on it and deep fry it, walleye tastes like McDonald's food. We had focused on fishing walleye because they paid the most.

But we had never fished over the limits set by the government. We paid very close attention to those limits, because when the limit was reached on any species, the entire lake shut down. So as we approached the limit on walleye, fishers would focus more on catching pike or whitefish.

The problem wasn't that we fished to the limit. The problem was the limit. In the 1990s an NDP government seeking re-election and needing northern votes arbitrarily doubled the commercial fishing limits across the North to entice fishers to vote for it. Problem was, there was no science to support doubling the limit. One by one, northerners fished out their lakes. First was Dore Lake, then Big Buffalo, then Deschambault, then Montreal. We paid the price for government folly.

Federally, the Conservatives under Stephen Harper were noted for their attacks on scientists. Sometimes it seems that the government doesn't want to know. After all, if you know, then you might have to address the problem.

There has been one study involving wolves in the fourteen years since Kenton Joel Carnegie was found not far from the Points North camp. The study wasn't about wolves. It was about caribou and included wolves merely because wolves eat caribou.

The Committee on the Status of Endangered Wildlife in Canada listed the woodland caribou as "threatened" under the *Species at Risk Act* in 2002. In 2012, Canada developed its *Recovery Strategy for the Woodland Caribou, Boreal Population, in Canada*. Saskatchewan is a signatory to the Accord for the Protection of Species at Risk and, under the accord, is responsible for creating a range plan for the woodland caribou.

Caribou across Canada are disappearing. The problem is that their habitat is being destroyed. Caribou do well only in places where there is no clear-cutting and where there are no roads, pipelines, or power lines dissecting the forest.

There is a small herd, maybe about thirty caribou, within a few kilometres of where I live. It is an area primarily of muskeg dotted with islands of pine and spruce forest. It is an area that the forestry companies have not gone into because the amount of wood available isn't worth the effort of building the necessary roads. It is safe only because the muskegs are too deep.

The muskeg also protects the caribou from wolves. In summer a caribou, with its long legs, can outrun a wolf here. In winter it's a different story. If the snow conditions are such that a crust forms on top, the wolves can run on top of the crust while the caribou break through.

The wolves in this territory move in cycles. When they move in, the moose move out. In the past few winters, there have been a lot of wolves in this region. When the moose move away, the wolves follow them. In a year or so the moose will come back and enjoy a few winters of quiet, and then the wolves will return.

Aboriginal Peoples have an inherent right as well as a Treaty right to hunt for food. However, no one bothers the caribou here. They are in an area where I trap and gather my firewood. In the past decade and a half, I have only tracked humans in that area a half dozen times, and it was usually people who remembered and followed a very old trail that connects the north end of Montreal Lake with the mostly abandoned community of Molanosa. The Cree in this area have stopped hunting caribou, not because of any change in the law, or any agreement with the governing bodies, but because we want them to survive.

If I am out cutting wood and find fresh caribou tracks, I leave that area alone for a couple of weeks until they have moved on. There is dwarf mistletoe here. It's a parasitic plant that kills pine, and dead pine makes great firewood. When the infection opens up the forest canopy, the moss the caribou prefer grows better in the newly available sunlight. Caribou find these areas to feed.

Government-mandated forestry practice, however, is to cut dwarf mistletoe whenever it is found near logging operations in the belief that its removal preserves the forest from a dreadful infection that kills trees. It seems that the government manages the forest for the forestry companies, not for the animals that live there.

We are frequently told not to worry about forestry operations—"the trees will grow back." But people who live out here know that even thirty years after a clear-cut and replanting, when the new trees are twenty feet tall, the animals stay away from those areas. Even the squirrels avoid them. And without squirrels, the martin and fisher also stay away. Yes, the trees grow back, but what then exists cannot be called a whole forest.

When asked about deforestation and old growth, the executive director of Saskatchewan's Forest Service Branch, Aaron Kuchirka, stated that "in some parts of Saskatchewan the forest has been harvested for the better part of a century and it would be hard to tell that it had ever been harvested." This is true. A century ago we harvested the forest by selective logging. Selective logging means going into the forest and selecting only those trees that are required and leaving everything else. Today those old cut areas remain as a whole forest; they are diverse and abundant in plants and animals. But about fifty years ago we began clear-cutting, and those newer cut areas are very visibly altered.

When asked about forest inventory—how much forest was left that hadn't been altered—Kuchirka replied, "Since the inventories were developed and paid for by the forest industry they typically will include information about forest age, species composition, and height." If the inventory of what's out there is determined by the forest industry, isn't it like getting the fox to count the chickens?

When pressed for a scientific explanation for current forestry practices, the government response is to rely upon the tired explanation that clear-cutting emulates natural disturbances. The problem is that there is nothing in nature that looks like a clear-cut. All of the pseudo-science around forestry is based on the idea that if clear-cuts are the same shape as forest fires, then they are natural. But a clear-cut and a forest fire share only a spatial resemblance. In early 2015 a large area of my nephew's trapline was clear-cut. A few months later, forest fires burned another very large area a few miles distant. The difference between the two areas is remarkable. In the area that burned in mid-summer, green plants began to reappear before autumn. Now the forest floor is completely covered in new growth. In the clear-cut areas, there is still virtually no regeneration. Clear-cuts might resemble forest fires spatially, but they do not compare in any other aspect.

The government and the forest industry frequently support the overharvest by promoting the idea that forest fires are a natural part of the ecosystem. Nearly every explanation of forestry practices will mention this supposed connection between forest fires and ecology. The intended inference is, of course, that clear-cutting is actually good for the forest and is somehow natural. The problem with this explanation is that forest fires have changed. Forest fires used to be primarily ground fires.

In this area there are many old cabin sites dating back over a hundred years. At many of these sites there are remnants of trenches that were dug around the periphery to protect the cabin from ground fires. It is only in the past fifty or so years that we began cutting fireguards, a swath of forest about a hundred metres wide, to protect property from crown fires—those that burn across the tops of forests.

Ground fires spread along the ground and burn the dead branches, needles, leaves, and bark shed by trees. They kill the undergrowth, small trees, moss, and shrubs, but not all of the large trees the way modern fires that climb up into the forest crown do. If modern forestry truly replicated natural fire, it would harvest only that part of the forest that fell to the forest floor.

Despite Saskatchewan's fame for its prairie and flatness, the province's northern half is forested—34 million hectares of forest, in fact, of which 11.7 million hectares are classified as commercial forest. The Far North region, the area around where the wolf attacks documented earlier occurred, is not commercial forest. That region has very poor soils, sometimes only a few centimetres thick, and the forest is thin and sparse. The main reason it is not included in the commercial zone is simply because it is too expensive to harvest. Trucking distances are too far, and the trees are too small.

The commercial zone is farther south on the boreal plain. This is the region where I grew up and continue to live. When I was seventeen and out working in the logging camps, I cut a white spruce that was fifty-nine inches (150 centimetres) across the stump. In the ensuing four and a half decades, I have not seen a tree that large again in this territory. There are very few trees left that are large enough to saw into lumber. The vast majority of larger trees have been taken.

The first highway in northern Saskatchewan was built between 1940 and 1948. It ended in La Ronge. Since the building of the highway in the 1940s, forestry companies have come into this territory. First they came for the saw logs. This was selective logging. They took the biggest, straightest trees and left everything else. The forest regrew. Then in the 1960s they came for the power poles and railroad ties, again logging selectively. Then in the late '70s and into the '80s they came for the pulp wood. But this time they clear-cut and took everything—size didn't matter, except in that larger trees were more economical to harvest. They sought the white spruce because of its fine grain and size and harvested it until very few white spruce remain.

Beginning in about 2000, they began coming for the fence posts and rails. I worry that in my children's and grandchildren's time, they will be coming for the chopsticks and toothpicks.

Saskatchewan has set an annual allowable cut in the commercial zone. It is currently set at 8.3 million cubic metres per year. The present rate of cutting uses 80 percent of the annual allowable cut, and Saskatchewan advertises that it has another 1.7 million cubic metres of wood available for any forestry company that wants to come here and cut it.

There are 8.3 million cubic metres of forest available, and the government won't tell us where it got that number from.

You'd think it would measure the forest, take an accurate inventory, and then determine how much that forest grows every year; revise that number based on the fact that, because of climate change and increased levels of carbon dioxide in the atmosphere, the forest may be growing faster; subtract from that number the areas taken by forest fires, diseases, insects, floods, droughts, and wind storms; and subtract another amount as a safety measure. Whatever was left over would make up the annual allowable cut.

But, no matter how many times Indigenous groups have asked the government, it won't tell us how it came up with the 8.3 million cubic metre annual allowable cut. We worry that this number is akin to the commercial fishing quota set by the NDP government two and a half decades ago and is more political than scientific.

At a public meeting concerning the caribou, we were told by government officials that they didn't know how many caribou there were in the region of commercial forestry. They didn't know what their range consisted of. They didn't know very much about the caribou because no one had taken the time to look. At present there are no plans to find out more. There are no studies scheduled. No new research has been planned. Nothing. The government doesn't know, and it is not concerned with finding out.

But, despite not knowing what range requirements are necessary to maintain the caribou we know to be here, they intend to keep clear-cutting the forest at the same or an accelerated rate. It seems the government doesn't want to know, because if it did, it would have to do something about it.

At the same caribou meeting mentioned above, I was in a side conversation with a senior government official asking him about the science behind caribou management and forestry operations. He told me that forestry was more of an art form than a science and seemed quite content with his answer: forestry just makes stuff up, writes it in a report, and doesn't study the results, and the government makes the practice into policy.

A few years ago, I asked the government for any studies done on the practice of scarifying on soils such as those on the boreal plain. Scarification is the act of dragging long, spiked anchor chains over the ground where clear-cutting has occurred. It is believed to help in regeneration. The government responded to my request by sending me a 1975 study, "An Appraisal of Natural Regeneration on Scarified Jack Pine Cutovers, Saskatchewan," by Jack Ball. The study details the growth rate on a variety of scarified plots. Its conclusion: scarification is a good thing. However, the study did not contain any control plots that had not been scarified. The author only looked at scarified plots and concluded that scarification was beneficial, that the trees grew back.

It would have been very interesting if the study had compared scarified plots to plots that had not been scarified and then compared those two plots to a plot where forest fire had occurred and determined which of the three plots regenerated most quickly and completely.

Even when the government does something that looks like science, the science is skewed to support the result preferred. In the above situation, the preferred result was to continue scarifying and continue the pretense that the forest was being maintained.

We call the wolf *Canis lupus*—*canis*, meaning from the dog or canine family; *lupus*, Latin for "wolf." It translates directly into Dog Wolf.

We call ourselves *Homo sapiens*. *Homo* denotes the hominid or human family. *Sapiens* is the Latin word for "wise."

More recently we have begun to refer to ourselves as *Homo sapiens sapiens*. So we are the wise, wise humans. Yet we do not behave that way.

There is evidence of *Homo sapiens* being on this planet for about 300,000 years. For 290,000 of those years we were hunter-gatherers and lived in close connection with an environment that included *Canis lupus*. About 10,000 years ago we entered what we refer to as the agricultural revolution. Shortly after we domesticated plants we began domesticating animals, primarily sheep and goats. We took the animals that the wolf normally ate and put a fence around them, which made them easier for the wolf to catch.

Then we went to war with the wolf.

Two hundred and fifty years ago, the Industrial Revolution gave us guns, steel traps, snares, and better poisons. By the mid-1970s, our wise human species had killed a large percentage of the wolves in North America. The only wolves to survive the slaughter were wolves that were timid and had learned to flee at the sight of *Homo sapiens*. Most of the human experience of wild wolves in the past half-century has been little more than a glimpse of the animal in the distance as it headed for thicker forest upon catching our scent.

It seems that phenomenon is beginning to change. We no longer have bounties on wolves, the government-sponsored eradication has come to an end, and the wolf population has grown and may now be at normal (if there is such a thing as normal anymore) levels. In some circumstances, the wolf in the distance is becoming less timid, perhaps because there have been sufficient generations that have not learned to fear humans.

Wolf-human interactions are increasing. As humans devour habitat—we are, after all, the world's greatest invasive species—the area available for the free-range wolf diminishes. If we expect to have wolves around for our children and grandchildren and great-grandchildren to experience, we have to leave space for them. And not just for the wolves; intact habitat is necessary for all species to survive, including the not-so-wise human species.

The Canadian boreal zone is one of the last remaining areas on the planet that survives as a whole forest, but we know next to nothing about it. Most of the money we have spent on research has gone into how to remove the trees. We don't know how many large herbivores like moose and caribou there are, and they should be the easiest to count because of their size. We don't know the quality of the water or the soils because we don't measure it. We haven't studied species such as the squirrel that are responsible for forest regeneration.

The insect population of the planet is declining rapidly. I took a road trip across the western United States and Canada last summer and rarely cleaned the windshield as I drove across the Dakotas, Montana, Utah, and Washington. Southern British Columbia and southern Alberta were the same. I did not begin to notice bugs on the windshield until I returned to the boreal region of northern Saskatchewan. The ecology is still healthy here. But, if we don't know about it, if we don't study it, if we don't use real science, how can we expect to keep it?

THE LAST WORD: WHAT THE ELDERS SAY

After being attacked by that wolf at the Key Lake mine in 1986, I spent a decade being nervous whenever I was in the forest—careful and alert, watching over my shoulder. The nervousness slowly diminished until I could be out there alone at night and not wonder how far away my gun was from where I was in my sleeping bag. Then, in 2006, the Carnegie family asked me to represent them at the coroner's inquest into the death of their son. A banker's box of material was delivered to my law office as disclosure. Included in the disclosure were two binders of photographs. One booklet contained all the photographs taken by Constable Noey of Kenton's body as he found it and photographs of the wolf tracks that tell the story of what happened to Kenton. The other booklet of photographs depicted the autopsy of Kenton.

I am now retired from law. I expect to never be in a courtroom again. I tell young lawyers and people who are in law school or intend to go to law school, "If you don't have to, don't look at the photographs. The judge has to look at them, but you don't."

It builds up over the decades. It's not any one set of photos, it's all of them, until a tiredness seeps into the body, the mind, and the soul. A job that used to be exciting becomes tiring and irritating.

But the two photo booklets in the Kenton Carnegie disclosure package were something even more for me. They awoke an old fear. Again when I walked a forest trail alone, I found myself repeatedly looking back, listening to every sound, feeling the need to carry either a walking stick or a gun.

My wife, Joan, worked in the law office with me. I told her she shouldn't look, but she did. We live two and a half kilometres from where we park our vehicles. In the winter, when the sun doesn't rise until nine-thirty and sets again at four-thirty, we walk in the dark going to and coming from work. It's a long walk when you are worried about wolves and see their fresh tracks in the snow. It began to bother her to make that walk.

Within days of concluding the inquest into the death of Kenton, we went to the Far North on a court matter. Joan had never been to the Far North, so we decided to make it a road trip so that she could experience the boreal shield. From La Ronge to Stony Rapids, Saskatchewan, is an eight-hour drive, a distance of 663 kilometres, and, incidentally, past the Points North camp, where we stopped for lunch. Seeing the place where Kenton had had his last meal, and hadn't made it back to for his next, put everything in perspective. The lake alongside which he went for a walk is not large. The place where they found him is within sight of the camp.

We arrived at about two in the afternoon. The lunch was over, and we were offered sandwiches. But I noticed that the buffet tables were still open. I asked, and they said I could help myself if I wanted, but the food was cold and they were about to clean it up. While eating the meal, I watched as the kitchen workers cleaned up the buffet table, knowing that all that leftover food that was being put into big black garbage bags was going to end up in the garbage dump where bears and ravens and foxes and wolves would find it.

My clients in Stony Rapids were an older couple who still lived out on the land. Joan immediately befriended the kind, constantly smiling woman. In their discussions Joan told this Elder Dene woman about her growing fear of wolves. The woman told her not to be afraid, that if she encountered a wolf she should remind it, "You are not supposed to eat me," and the wolf would leave her alone.

When Joan told me this, I was reminded of what Rosalie Tsannie-Burseth had told me her father, a Dene Elder, said about the wolves that attacked Kenton. He said those wolves must be young wolves that don't know the proper way to behave and, like teenagers, go out and get themselves into trouble.

Then I read Adam Weymouth's *Kings of the Yukon: An Alaskan River Journey*, in which he interviews Tr'ondëk Hwëch'in Elder Percy Henry. Percy was eighty-nine years old at the time and had received his education on the land:

> "They're finding a lot of caribou dying, because the doctor quit bothering with them."
>
> "Who's the doctor?" I say.
>
> "The wolf is the doctor of all animals," he says. "He chase caribou. He don't kill 'em right there. He could. But his mother train him, you don't kill 'em till one falls aside. That's a weak one. So that's how they stay healthy. Make 'em sweat. You see that Yellowstone Park. Animal there were half dead. So they took some wolf in there and all the animal were happy. Bring their life back to where it should be."
>
> But now, Percy says, the young wolves don't know what to do. It began when the state started culling wolves as a way of protecting caribou. They shot the old wolves, the ones that train the pups. Now Percy sees wolves coming into yards to attack dogs, he sees wolves chasing skidoos. They haven't been taught fear; they've had no education from their elders.

There's no doubt that the massive kill of wolves during the past century had an incredible impact on the wolf, and not only on its numbers. The wolf's genetics have been changed because breeding was reduced to a less-diverse, shrunken population.

We are in a new time, with new challenges. If *Homo sapiens sapiens* are going to survive into the future, it will not be because we are so smart and have developed technology. We will survive the way we always have, dependent upon the ecosystem to give us air, water, and food. Saving the ecosystem, which includes the wolf, saves ourselves. The future of *Homo sapiens sapiens* and *Canis lupus* are tied together. It's our job to figure out how our two species share this planet.

WORKS CITED

Ball, W.J. *An Appraisal of Natural Regeneration on Scarified Jack Pine Cutovers, Saskatchewan.* Information report NOR-X-136. Northern Forest Research Centre, Canadian Forest Service, Environment Canada, Edmonton, April 1975. http://cfs.nrcan. gc.ca/pubwarehouse/pdfs/11574.pdf.

Bibikov, Dimitri Ivanovic. *Der Wolf (Canis lupus).* Wittenberg: A. Ziemsen Verlag, 1988.

Environment Canada. *Recovery Strategy for the Woodland Caribou (Rangifer tarandus caribou), Boreal Population, in Canada.* Species at Risk Act Recovery Strategy Series. Ottawa, 2012. http://publications.gc.ca/site/eng/9.574049/publication.html.

Geist, Valerius. "When Do Wolves Become Dangerous to Humans?" Unpublished draft, September 29, 2007. http://www. idahoforwildlife.com/files/pdf/drGeist/When_do_wolves_ become_dangerous_to_humans.pdf.

Herrero, Stephen. *Bear Attacks: Their Causes and Avoidance.* New York: Nick Lyons Books/Winchester Press, 1985.

Johnson, Harold R. *Firewater: How Alcohol Is Killing My People (and Yours).* Regina: University of Regina Press, 2016.

Linnell, John D.C., and Julien Alleau. "Predators that Kill Humans: Myth, Reality, Context and the Politics of Wolf Attacks on People." In *Problematic Wildlife: A Cross-Disciplinary Approach*, edited by Francesco M. Angelici, 357–71. Cham, Switzerland: Springer, 2016.

McNay, M.E. "A Case History of Wolf-Human Encounters in Alaska and Canada." Wildlife technical bulletin no. 13, Alaska Department of Fish and Game, Juneau, 2002. 44 pp.

———. "A Review of Evidence and Findings Related to the Death of Kenton Carnegie on November 8, 2005 Near Points North, Saskatchewan." Alaska Department of Fish and Game, Fairbanks, 2007.

———. "Wolf-Human Interactions in Alaska and Canada: A Review of the Case History." *Wildlife Society Bulletin* 30, no. 3 (2002): 831–43.

McNay, M.E., and P.W. Mooney. "Attempted Predation of a Child by a Gray Wolf, *Canis Lupus*, near Icy Bay, Alaska." *Canadian Field-Naturalist* 119, no. 2 (2005): 197–201.

Mowat, Farley. *Never Cry Wolf*. Toronto: McClelland & Stewart, 1963.

Paquet, P.C., and E.G. Walker. 2006. "Review of Investigative Findings Relating to the Death of Kenton Carnegie at Points North, Saskatchewan." Prepared for and submitted to Office of the Chief Coroner, Saskatchewan Justice, Regina. 32 pp.

Rowling, J.K. "History of Magic in North America." Pottermore.com, March 2016, https://www.pottermore.com/collection-episodic/history-of-magic-in-north-america-en.

"Shadow Stalkers." Episode 6 of *Hunter Hunted*, season 2. Written by Geoffrey Luck, featuring Gary Haynes. Aired July 24, 2006, on National Geographic Television. 46 minutes.

Weymouth, Adam. *Kings of the Yukon: An Alaskan River Journey*. London: Particular Books, 2018.

INDEX

Page numbers in *italics* represent photos/illustrations.

wolves *(continued)*: McCallum
attack, 89; myths of, 99,
107, 111, 114; overview
of, 113–14; Points North
dump/kitchen, 33, 95,
101; Svarckopf and Van
Galder attack, 20–2; tracks
of, 36, *37*, *57*, 58–60, *59*;
in Uranium City, 40;
vocalizations, 112
wolves and Carnegie attack:
body consumption, 73–5,
84–6; body dragging,
69–73, 75–7; body injuries,
83, 88–9, 90–2; body
moved, 36; body position,

61–2; clothing at scene,
63–6, *65*, 67–8; finding
body, 29–31, 32, 36, 38;
Noey's nightmares, 41;
overview, 79; tracks and
snow, *37–8*, *47*, *51*; tracks of,
56–8, 60–1, 72, 104–5; and
truth, xv–xvi; wolf attack
conclusion, 99, 104–6;
wolf scat, 106; wolves as
inexperienced, 137–8. *See
also* death scene; death
scene, photos; Paquet-
Walker report
Wong, Edmond T., 44

ABOUT THE AUTHOR

Harold R. Johnson is the author of five works of fiction and three works of nonfiction. His most recent books include *Peace and Good Order: The Case for Indigenous Justice in Canada*; *Clifford: A Memoir, A Fiction, A Fantasy, A Thought Experiment*; and *Firewater: How Alcohol Is Killing My People (and Yours)*, which was a finalist for the Governor General's Literary Award for Nonfiction. Born and raised in northern Saskatchewan to a Swedish father and a Cree mother, Johnson is a graduate of Harvard Law School and managed a private practice for several years before becoming a Crown prosecutor. He is a member of the Montreal Lake Cree Nation and lives in northern Saskatchewan with his wife, Joan.